World Food Policy

Also from Westphalia Press

westphaliapress.org

The Idea of the Digital University

France and New England Volumes 1, 2, & 3

Treasures of London

The History of Photography

L'Enfant and the Freemasons

Baronial Bedrooms

Making Trouble for Muslims

Material History and Ritual Objects

Paddle Your Own Canoe

Opportunity and Horatio Alger

Careers in the Face of Challenge

Bookplates of the Kings

Collecting American Presidential Autographs

Freemasonry in Old Buffalo

Young Freemasons?

Social Satire and the Modern Novel

The Essence of Harvard

Ivanhoe Masonic Quartettes

A Definitive Commentary on Bookplates

James Martineau and Rebuilding Theology

No Bird Lacks Feathers

Gilded Play

Earthworms, Horses, and Living Things

The Man Who Killed President Garfield

Anti-Masonry and the Murder of Morgan

Understanding Art

Homeopathy

Fishing the Florida Keys

Collecting Old Books

Masonic Secret Signs and Passwords

The Thomas Starr King Dispute

Earl Warren's Masonic Lodge

Lariats and Lassos

Mr. Garfield of Ohio

The Wisdom of Thomas Starr King

The French Foreign Legion

War in Syria

Naturism Comes to the United States

New Sources on Women and Freemasonry

Designing, Adapting, Strategizing in Online Education

Gunboat and Gun-runner

Meeting Minutes of Naval Lodge No. 4 F.A.A.M

World Food Policy

Volume 1, Number 1, Spring 2014

Edited by Keokam Kraisoraphong

WESTPHALIA PRESS
An imprint of Policy Studies Organization

World Food Policy: Volume 1, Number 1, 2014

Westphalia Press
An imprint of Policy Studies Organization
1527 New Hampshire Ave., NW
Washington, D.C. 20036
dgutierrezs@ipsonet.org

ISBN-13: 978-1935907831
ISBN-10: 1935907832

Updated material and comments on this edition
can be found at the Westphalia Press website:
www.westphaliapress.org

Volume 1, Number 1 • Spring 2014

World Food Policy
(WFP)
A Journal of the Policy Studies Organization
In Collaboration with
The Royal Institute of Thailand

World Food Policy (WFP) semi-annually publishes research-based articles exploring various aspects of policies and decisions that affect food systems at the global, regional and transnational levels. Articles on policies pertaining to non-food commodities with noticeable impact on the world food sector or comparative national food policies are also within the scope of the journal.

The aim of ***WFP*** is to promote a multi-disciplinary forum for generating the analysis and understanding of global trends as well as regional and local forces shaping food and food policies around the world. The editors warmly invite submissions at: wfp.editorial@gmail.com
Please visit ***WFP*** website: http://www.ipsonet.org/publications/open-access/world-food-policy

Statements of fact, argument or policy advocacy in ***World Food Policy*** (***WFP***) are solely those of the authors and do not imply endorsement by the editors or publisher.

®
Logo and Cover Design
Kornkamol Bunnag

Editor's Note

Under the editorial sponsorship of the Royal Institute of Thailand, ***World Food Policy (WFP)*** is published by the Policy Studies Organization (PSO), as part of the PSO's effort to disseminate scholarship and information to serve those making, evaluating and studying policies in the food sector.

WFP welcomes articles, which explore various aspects of policies and decisions that affect food systems at the global, regional and transnational levels, including comparative national food policies and policies pertaining to non-food commodities with noticeable impact on the world food markets.

The editorial process of ***WFP*** is overseen by an international editorial board of renowned experts in different fields to ensure the publication of a scholarly peer-reviewed, multidisciplinary journal. Communicability among scholars and practitioners from various disciplines and sectors is the guiding principle in the selection and editing of papers to be published in the journal. Rigor will not be sacrificed, but technical jargons specific to any particular field and mathematical expressions (beyond simple equations) should be avoided, and if absolutely unavoidable, should be carefully explained. Articles while based on sound analysis should provide insights useful for practical policy making.

To launch the journal, ***WFP*** has invited a number of leading scholars to write for the first two inaugural issues. This first one will look at the food sector from global perspectives, while the next one, to be published in the autumn of 2014, explores food policies from regional and national perspectives. ***WFP*** will accept submissions of papers for subsequent issues, beginning with ***WFP*** volume 2, number 1, Spring 2015.

The editors hope that ***WFP*** will help provide a multi-disciplinary forum for generating the analysis and understanding of global trends as well as regional and local forces shaping food and food policies around the world.

IFPRI's Mark Rosegrant Remembers Robert E. Evenson, Professor Emeritus of Economics, Yale University

Bob Evenson died on February 2, 2013.

I first met Bob in 1976 in Los Banos, Philippines, where he was an Agricultural Development Council associate and visiting professor at the University of the Philippines and I was the greenest of green PhD students sitting in a cubicle at the International Rice Research Institute (IRRI) doing the field research for my dissertation from the University of Michigan. Bob was already an established scholar, but he treated me with dignity and respect (and probably mild amusement at some of my questions).

Gentle (but rigorous!) mentorship was Bob's hallmark; he was a great teacher and advisor to hundreds of students at Yale and elsewhere, many of whom have gone on to highly successful careers. Bob was a leading scholar in many areas of research related to agricultural research, economic development, and education.

Coming from a farming background himself, Bob's passion was improving the well-being of poor farmers in developing countries, and his research was filled with insights on how to do this. His work on the determinants of agricultural productivity research and the economic returns to agricultural research was pioneering, and remained a core interest throughout his career. It was my good fortune to work with him on these issues in the late 1980s and 1990s and into the 2000s. Even when I wasn't working with him, I could always call him up for help when facing a difficult research issues. Bob's patented long and rambling answers were seminars in themselves, but invariably ended up helping me through the problem. I have lost a great friend and mentor, and the world of research and agricultural development has lost a champion.

Mark Rosegrant
Director
Environment and Production Technology Division
International Food Policy Research Institute
Washington, DC

World Food Policy (*WFP*)
Volume 1 Number 1 Spring 2014

Table of Contents

Food Policy as a Wicked Problem: Contending with Multiple Demands and Actors

B. Guy Peters[1] and Jon Pierre[2]

Solving any policy problem is difficult but some are more difficult than are others. As food becomes a more central political issue the underlying conflicts between actors–producers and consumers, GMO producers and opponents, etc.–become more apparent and more intensely politicized. Further, food policy becomes more difficult to discuss independently and becomes embedded in other policy debates such as those over water, population and climate change. This paper conceptualizes food policy as a "wicked problem" and discusses how this concept originally derived from the planning literature illuminates the difficulties involved in making contemporary food policy.

Keywords: wicked problem, food security, unanticipated consequences, social complexity

Providing adequate, safe, and nutritious food has always been a crucial demand on society, and on government, but that demand continues to become more difficult. The capacity to provide food for the people of the world is threatened by a number of factors. Perhaps the most obvious of those factors is simply that there are more of those people to feed. With current rates of population growth approximately 40,000 more people each day must be fed. And those people are not distributed evenly, but population tends to be increasing in countries that already face severe challenges in feeding their populations.

The effects of population increases are to some extent being compounded by the significant successes in economic and social policies in reducing extreme poverty (Ravallion 2013). Obviously increasing the consumption of millions of people who lived in abject poverty is a triumph for humanitarian policies, but it also means that these people will place greater demand on the system for food production. And the increased demand may be greatest for products like meat that require the greatest inputs, and hence will create additional strains on production.

At the same time that the population is increasing many of the factors needed for food production are being even more strained. Many areas that are important for food production are now in persistent drought, and groundwater resources are being exhausted (Wines 2013). In addition to the strain on water resources that results in part from climate change, that change also influences the viability of many traditional agricultural regions. Crops that once may have grown well, e.g., wheat in the southern plains in the United States, may no longer be viable because of increasing temperatures. While other crops may become viable in those regions, the produc-

[1] Maurice Falk Professor of American Government, the Department of Political Science, University of Pittsburgh, USA.

[2] Department of Political Science, Gothenburg University, Sweden.

tion of important cereal crops like wheat and maize appears increasingly threatened. And as the same time that water resources are being exhausted, the land necessary to grow food is also being depleted (Johnson and Lewis 2007).

The problems mentioned above concern primarily the basic issue of matching production to consumption. For more affluent areas of the globe other food policy issues have become more apparent, especially questions of quality and safety. Although food borne diseases are perhaps less common in real terms than in the past, they are now more on the political radar and demand more public policy intervention. Beginning at least with Mad Cow Disease in the UK (Ratzan 1998; van Zwanenberg and Millstone 2006) most developed economies have had a series of significant food scares that have demanded large-scale intervention by government, and also changes in food policy. In humanitarian terms these diseases of affluence may not be as significant as those of poverty, but they still cost lives and damage health.

Food Policy as a Policy Problem: Is it a Wicked Problem?

The introduction above raises some of the most fundamental and obvious questions about food policy, but this policy area (like many others) is complex and has a number of dimensions. Indeed, we can characterize food policy as a "wicked problem", emphasizing the multi-dimensionality of the issues involved and the numerous internal conflicts and contradictions that may arise when attempting to "solve" the issue. Food policy means many different things to different people and we need to have some grasp of the technological and political complexity involved to understand its dynamics.

The Nature of Wicked Problems

The term "wicked problem" was developed by two planners (Rittel and Webber 1973) to describe policy issues that did not fit neatly into the rather linear and constrained logic of most planning and policymaking (see also Peters and Hoornbeek 2005). As described in the original paper and in subsequent attempts to understand issues of this type (see APSC 2007), wicked problems have the following characteristics:

(1) these problems are difficult to define;
(2) these problems involve multiple interdependencies and are often multi-causal;
(3) attempts to solve wicked problems often have unforseen consequences (see Sieber 1980); and
(4) wicked problems are socially complex.

Contemporary food policy has many if not all of these characteristics, and some of the political and social complexity involved in the policy can be understood through utilizing this framework for analysis.

Defining the Issues

At its most basic level, food policy is simple—it is policy concerning the production and distribution of food. But that conception of food policy is deceptively simple and as soon as we begin to examine the political and social dimensions then a number of vexing questions arise. Some of these questions are "merely political", but some address deeply held convictions and cultural norms that pose particularly difficult problems for those in government attempting to solve them. The fundamental political question is how to frame the policy issue in ways that can be addressed effectively through the political system (Chong and Druckman 2007).

The first point to consider is that food policy is about more than production, it also involves issues of food safety, distribution, allocation, and consumption. For the affluent countries of Europe, North America, and the Antipodes (as well as some areas of some other countries) the first policy issue that people would think about concerning food is not whether there is enough but rather the purity and safety of the large quantities available to them. Everything else being equal, an emphasis on safety will tend to reduce levels of production, given the investments required in controlling potential infections, refrigeration, and monitoring production.

The production of food also raises other safety questions, at least in the minds of critics of the contemporary food production system. It is clear that total food production could be increased by the use of genetically modified crops, or GMOs. These crops are used extensively in the United States and Brazil, but their planting continues to be banned in Europe. The ban in Europe is based on the "precautionary principle", meaning that it is best not to undertake policy interventions if there are substantial risks of unintended consequences (Majone 2002). Further, imports of food raised from GMO seeds, or containing other banned substances are also prohibited.

These constraints on crop production point to yet another of the definitional problems contained within food policy. For one set of actors involved in food policy the goal is production, while for others the goal is consumption. This real conflict in goals arises in the issue of food safety above, but is perhaps seen most clearly in setting prices on a world market. The agricultural policies of many countries, and perhaps especially the United States and the European Union, are directed more at the producers of food than at the consumers of that food (Alston and Sumner 2007). International organizations attempt to intervene to create greater food security for less-developed systems, but are constrained by the role of markets, and particularly subsidized markets, in setting prices.

The contrast between the consumption demands of the more affluent regions of the world and the consumption needs of less-developed reasons is emphasized in the emergence of obesity as a policy issue in many industrialized countries (Lang and Rayner 2005). Not only does the spread of obesity, especially among children, reflect the availability of plentiful food, it also reflects changes in the marketing of food and consumption patterns. With the use of ingredients such as high fructose corn syrup it becomes possible for people, and again especially children, to become obese while being malnourished.

In a larger context we also see that the key linkage between the producers and the consumers of food—the domestic and international markets—have been seriously malfunctioning for decades. Many developed countries still use tariffs to protect their domestic agricultural sector from competition from developing countries. In the EU, support to the agricultural sector is along with the structural funds the most costly item in the budget, yet (or perhaps because as a result) the relationship between demand and supply is extremely weak. This leads to periodic over-production of specific items—we need to only think of the "butter mountain" or the "wine lake" in Europe—alongside continuing famine in other parts of the world. If we bring in these aspects of the food market into the larger context of food policy, its "wicked" nature becomes even clearer.

Interdependencies and Conflicts

The most fundamental conflict in food policy is between producers and consumers, as implied above. Consumers want plentiful and inexpensive food, while producers want a stable and substantial income for their efforts. In subsistence agriculture these two actors are the same so the conflict is minimal, but in industrial agriculture there is a conflict, often seen in government policies. For example, the Common Agricultural Policy in the European Union provides substantial support to farmers, but those subsidies in turn increases food prices within Europe (Grant 1997).

Many other interdependencies and conflicts involved with food policy have already been mentioned, but there is one other that has become a source of political concern, and has to some extent therefore affected the manner in which other aspects of food policy are made and implemented. Food policy has increasingly come to be defined as security policy. This equation of food with security has been expressed by the Food and Agriculture Organization, the World Health Organization, and other humanitarian organizations more on the individual level (FAO 2006) but countries have also begun to conceptualize food policy as a component of their national security policy.

But food security is not only an issue for individuals, it is also defined in national terms and as a component of national security, just as has energy policy (Shirer 2011; Newman 2010). This conception of food security involves first that the individual national can feed its own population through its own internal production, and therefore does not depend on other, potentially antagonistic countries for something as basic as food. This notion also implies that ensuring food security also prevents unrest in poorer countries that can pose a more militarized threat to national security.

Food policy is also interdependent with trade policy in the increasingly globalized system of food production. At the extreme, the Doha Round of negotiations within the Word Trade Organization encountered severe difficulties over agricultural trade (Polaski 2008). Agricultural producing countries such as the United States, Brazil, and Australia have different priorities in trade than do importing countries, and therefore trade negotiations are crucial for the ability of importing countries. Further, food safety issues become involved in trade negotiations and can become non-tariff barriers to exporting for less-developed countries (Otsuki, Wilson, and Sewadeh 2001).

In the industrialized economies perhaps the major conflict over the nature of agriculture policy comes from environmentalists. Agriculture produces a number of significant environmental problems, especially the industrial style of farming found in many developed or transitional economies. The number of environmental problems created are too numerous to detail here, but the basic point is that high volume agriculture generally encounters conflicts with environmental goals. For example, high volume agriculture tends to use numerous chemical fertilizers that then run off into water supplies, producing algae blooms and then exhaustion of dissolved oxygen when the algae die. And further chemical pesticides used in large-scale commercial farming get into the food chain affecting animals and humans.

Large-scale agriculture is also a major consumer of fossil fuels. This fuel use is not only for powering farm equipment but also for manufacturing the fertilizers and pesticides used in factory farming. The globalization of agriculture also means that large volumes of food are shipped around the globe, often with a very large carbon footprint. During the winter Americans want blackberries, and Europeans want fresh melons. These foods can be provided from countries in Latin America and Africa, or perhaps even Asia, but at a very high energy and economic cost.

The capacity to convert food crops and land to energy production represents yet another of the contradictions and trade-offs involved in food and agriculture policy. While ethanol and bio-diesel are seen by some as a sustainable remedy for energy shortages, diversion of land from food disadvantages the poor while advantaging more affluent automobile owners. Thus, it is impossible to make good choices about either agriculture policy or energy policy without considering their impacts on one another, and other policy areas.

Unanticipated Consequences

Another defining feature of wicked problems is that introducing policies to solve them tend to have unforseen consequences (Sieber 1980) and may indeed often end up exacerbating those problems. Classical examples would include tampering with nature by bringing in species to solve problems of overpopulation of other species. With no natural enemy in their new habitats the imported species multiplies and ends up causing a problem even bigger than the original one.

In policy terms, unanticipated consequences are sometimes not entirely unpredictable, yet the policy process fails to anticipate the new problems. For instance, changing a tax system so that it incentivizes women to enter the labor market will dramatically increase the demand on (public or private) daycare for small children. Similarly, increasing taxes and charges on high-fat food items as has sometimes been suggested may drive consumers not to look for more low-fat food items but instead towards even more hazardous food. Regulations urging schools to offer children a healthy meal may have the unintended consequence of either kids heading over to a nearby hamburger restaurant or bringing junk food with them to school.

The key point here is that public policy or regulations are implemented in a dynamic social context and as a result it is often extremely difficult to predict the outcomes of such reform. Wicked problems are extraordinarily challenging in this respect as their multidimensional and complex character basically makes prediction about outcomes impossible, and therefore make unintended consequences more probable.

Social Complexity

Food policy also touches upon a number of social issues that need to be considered in order to understand the dynamics of this policy. Many of these social issues arise because agriculture involves land, and land owning is far from evenly distributed by caste, class, or gender. Further, different types of crops tend to be controlled by different social groups, with women tending to control their own gardens and perhaps small animals but men controlling most cash crops (Mammen and Paxson 2000). As well as affecting the roles of women, landholding patterns also tend to perpetuate control of dominant ethnic groups and exclude many would-be entrepreneurs within developing economies.[3]

[3] The redistribution of agricultural land was central to the settlement between the FARC and the government of Colombia (Brodzinsky 2013). This settlement should permit millions of previously landless peasants to acquire some rights to the land they have been working.

The issue raised above concerning the potential for GMO crops to increase production significantly, and the resistance to those crops, points to another interdependency in food policy, namely the relationship with intellectual property rights. As well as facing resistance from environmentalists and food safety advocates, GMO crops have faced complaints because the large agricultural firms that have developed these crops are using their patents to ensure high levels of profit.[4] Thus, this version of progress in agriculture raises fundamental issues of justice and economic equality at the same time it raises environmental issues.

Indeed, the market nature of agriculture in the contemporary world raises numerous questions of this type. The cultural image of the farmer is generally that of the "yeoman farmer" working his (or her) fields as an individual and being close to the land.[5] The contemporary reality is corporate agriculture with massive industrial operations covering thousands of acres or process thousands of animals in a limited space. The marketized version of agriculture in much of the West, as well as in countries such as Brazil, Russia, and Argentina, raise many of the same questions about economic justice and the role of markets in a fundamental area of human existence such as foods raised by GMO crops. History provides only too many examples of food and agricultural policy as a massive market failure. It is also to some extent a political failure as political institutions and actors have become captives of powerful organized interests protecting the agricultural constituencies in the developing countries.

[4] The producers of genetically modified seed generally prohibit farmers from retaining seed from one year's crop to plant the next year, thus assuring sales the following year. This was not true for other improved strains of crops produced by cross-breeding rather than genetic manipulation.

[5] For one description see Cash (1941).

The social dimension of land ownership and therefore of food policy intensifies the complexity of the policy. Attempts to enhance production may concentrate land and power in the hands of the agri-businesses. This will also shift production away from traditional and perhaps more sustainable crops to cash crops, that often may well be exported. Thus, yet another internal contradiction and irony of policy may arise. While fostering export agriculture may assist in economic development in some senses it may also undermine existing patterns of food production and significantly harm subsistence farming.

The epidemic of obesity mentioned above also reflects fundamental social and cultural changes in food consumption, and to some extent in food policy. The emphasis on processed foods in the food industry, e.g., high-fructose corn syrup as opposed to more natural sugars, has been subsidized in part by agricultural policies. And the widespread availability of snack foods has tended to decrease emphasis on cooking more nutritious meals at home, affecting not only food consumption but also social patterns.

How to Cope With Wickedness?

The above discussion has presented a rather dismal view for policy analysts. Food policy appears at first glance to be a relatively simple question about finding ways to raise and distribute enough food for the growing population of the world. But when the policy is considered more carefully there are a number of interactions with, and contradictions to, other policy area. Perhaps more fundamentally, defining food policy involves a number of dimensions and alternative frames each of which produce different conceptions and different priorities.

Are there ways of cutting through this complexity and finding ways of making less ambiguous judgments about this policy area? Perhaps the most appealing means of addressing these conundrums is to have a clearer sense of the policy and social priorities that should be pursued. For example, for major international organizations such as the Food and Agriculture Organization production and individual food security are central values, although many of the other concerns are acknowledged. But the candidates for priorities may well depend upon levels of economic development and position in world markets.

Another approach to coping with the complexity involved in food policy may be through attempting to find some encompassing concept that can address many, if perhaps not all, of the seemingly contradictory issues raised above. The idea of *sustainability* may be an appropriate concept for that purpose. It addresses not only the need to sustain the individuals who require food but also to sustain the environment that can be adversely affected by industrialized agriculture. It can also address, albeit perhaps tangentially, the potential social consequences of changing forms of food production.

References

Alston, J.M., and D.A. Sumner. 2007. "Perspectives on Farm Policy Reform." *Journal of Agricultural and Resource Economics* 32: 1-19.

Australian Public Services Commission (APSC). 2007. *Tackling Wicked Problems: A Public Policy Perspective.* Canberra: Commonwealth Government.

Brodzinsky, S. 2013. "FARC Peace Talks: Colombia Unveils Major Breakthrough." *The Guardian*, May 27.

Cash, W.J. 1941. *The Mind of the South.* New York: Vintage Books.

Chong, D., and J.N. Druckman. 2007. "Framing Theory." *Annual Review of Political Science* 10: 103-26.

Food and Agriculture Organization. 2006. *Policy Brief: Food Security.* Rome: Food and Agriculture Organization, June.

Grant, W. 1997. *Common Agriculture Policy.* New York: ST. Martin's.

Johnson D.L., and L.A. Lewis. 2007. *Land Degradation: Creation and Destruction.* Oxford: Oxford University Press.

Lang, T., and G. Rayner. 2005. "Obesity: A Growing Issue for European Policy." *Journal of European Social Policy* 15: 301-27.

Majone, G. 2002. "The Precautionary Principle and its Policy Implications." *Journal of Common Market Studies* 40: 89-109.

Mammen, K., and C. Paxson. 2000. "Women's Work and Economic Development." *Journal of Economic Perspectives* 14: 141-64.

Newman, E. 2010. "Critical Human Security Studies." *Review of International Studies* 36: 77-94.

Otsuki, T., J.S. Wilson, and M. Sewadeh. 2001. "Saving Two in a Billion: Quantifying the Trade Effects of European Food Safety Standards on African Exports." *Food Policy* 26: 496-514.

Peters, B.G., and J.A. Hornbeek. 2005. "The Problem of Policy Problems." *Journal of Comparative Policy Analysis* 7: 349-70.

Polaski, S. 2008. "Rising Food Prices, Poverty and the Doha Round, Policy Outlook." *The Carnegie Endowment*, May 21.

Ratzan, S. 1998. *Mad Cow Crisis: Health and the Public Good. London*: UCL Press.

Ravallion, M. 2013. "How Long Will it Take to Lift One Billion People Out of Poverty?" Policy Research Working Paper 6325. Washington, DC: The World Bank.

Rittel, H, W.J., and M.M. Webber. 1973. "Dilemmas in the General Theory of Planning." *Policy Sciences* 4: 155-69.

Shirer, J. 2011. *Food Security Contributes to National Security, DIPNOTES*. US State Department Blog, October 26.

Sieber, S. 1980. *Fatal Remedies: The Ironies of Social Intervention*. New York: Plenum.

van Zwanenberg, P., and E. Millstone. 2006. *BSE: Risk, Science and Governance*. Oxford: Oxford University Press.

Wines, M. 2013. "Wells Dry, Fertile Plains Turn to Dust." *The New York Times*, May 19. Accessed May 20. http://www.nytimes.com/2013/05/20/us/high-plains-aquifer-dwindles-hurting-farmers.html?pagewanted=all&_r=0.

Food Price and Trade Policy Evolution Since the 1950s: A Global Perspective[1]

Kym Anderson[2]

In both rich and poor countries, food markets have been subjected to some of the most heavy-handed governmental interventions. Policy developments in this sector since the 1950s have been mostly gradual but persistent, involving in many cases a change from taxing to subsidizing farmers—and from subsidizing to taxing food consumers—as national per capita incomes grow. In a few important countries there also have been transformational policy reforms, and in all countries there tends to be only partial short-run transmission of international price fluctuations to domestic markets—a tendency that has not declined over time. This paper summarizes indicators of these trends and fluctuations in price-distorting impacts of policies for a sample of 82 countries, using a global set of annual data from 1955 to 2011. It then draws implications for what policy interventions might evolve over coming years, especially as emerging economies attain and move beyond middle-income status.

JEL codes: F13, F14, N50, Q17, Q18

Keywords: Distortions to food markets, nominal rate of assistance, welfare reduction index

Introduction

Agricultural and food industries have been subjected throughout history to perhaps more governmental interventions than any other sector of national economies. As of 2004, agricultural trade-related policies are estimated to account for 70 percent of the global welfare cost of the world's merchandise trade distortions, even though the agricultural sector contributes only 6 percent of global trade and 3 percent of global GDP (Anderson, Cockburn, and Martin 2010, Table 2.3).

For advanced economies, the most commonly articulated reason to restrict food trade has been to protect domestic producers from import competition as they come under competitive pressure to shed labor. Such measures harm not only domestic food consumers and exporters of other products but also foreign producers and traders of food products. For decades, agricultural protection and subsidies in high-income (and some middle-income) countries have depressed international prices of farm products, lowering the earnings of farmers and associated rural businesses in developing countries.

Meanwhile, developing countries' policies have further depressed the price incentives for their farmers, thus exacerbating the deleterious effects on them of the richer

[1] This paper draws on one section of a recent survey, co-authored by Gordon Rausser and Johan Swinnen, published in the June 2013 issues of the Journal of Economic Literature. I thank those co-authors for their insights, and also Signe Nelgen for assistance with the figures and tables. Financial support from the Australian Research Council and Rural Industries Research and Development Corporation is also gratefully acknowledged.

[2] George Gollin Professor of Economics, School of Economics, University of Adelaide; CEPR Fellow; and Professor of Economics, Arndt-Corden Department of Economics, Australian National University, Canberra.

countries' farm policies. Governments of many developing countries have taxed their farmers more heavily than producers in other sectors. As well, many developing countries chose to overvalue their currency and to pursue an import-substituting industrialization strategy by restricting imports of manufactures. Together, these measures have indirectly taxed net sellers of food in developing economies, while effectively subsidizing those countries' net buyers of food.

These policies mean there has been overproduction of food in high-income countries and underproduction in low-income countries. They also mean there has been less international food trade than would have been the case under free trade. The end result is thinner and thus more volatile markets for these weather-dependent products.

Food policies became newsworthy during 2008–12 because international food prices spiked upwards three times in that period. These price spikes have been caused partly by biofuel policies, but they have been exacerbated by the grain trade-policy responses of numerous countries at a time of low global grain stocks. Responses by food-surplus developing countries typically involved restrictions on exports, while those by food-deficit developing countries involved a lowering of import barriers. The policymakers' ostensible motivation for these variations in border restrictions—which have also occurred in previous price-spike periods—has been to prevent a decline in national food security: each country has aimed to protect its domestic food consumers (and indirectly, to protect the current government from losing power). Together, however, these measures have amplified international price spikes so that each country's measures have harmed other countries' food consumers (Carter et al. 2011; Martin and Anderson 2012; Anderson and Nelgen 2012).

Some agricultural- and trade-policy developments of the past half-century have happened quite suddenly and been transformational. Such events include decolonization in Africa and elsewhere around 1960; the creation of the Common Agricultural Policy (CAP) in Europe in 1962; the introduction of flexible exchange rates from the 1970s; liberalization, deregulation, privatization, and democratization in many countries from the mid-1980s; the opening of markets in China in 1979, in Vietnam in 1986, and in Eastern Europe (following the fall of the Berlin Wall) in 1989; and the demise of the Soviet Union in 1991.

However, dominating the post World War II period are the influences in sovereign states of policies that change gradually in the course of economic development, as incomes grow and comparative advantages evolve. These trends, and the above-mentioned turning points, are revealed in a global five-decade database of evidence recently compiled by the World Bank. That database also exposes both the extent to which recent agricultural policy reforms have succeeded in reversing prior policy trends, and an emergence of agricultural protection in middle-income countries.

The next section of the paper outlines the database and its various empirical indicators of policy induced price distortions in national markets of both high-income and developing countries. The following section summarizes the trends and fluctuations in those indicator estimates. The final section draws implications for what policy interventions might evolve over coming years, especially as emerging economies attain and move beyond middle-income status.

Database and Indicators of Price Distortions

Empirical indicators of food and agricultural price-distorting policies have been provided annually since the late 1980s by the Secretariat of the OECD (Organization of Economic Co-operation and Development) (2012a) for its 30 member countries. They have become known as Producer and Consumer Support Estimates, or PSEs and CSEs. The OECD also has released PSEs and CSEs for Brazil, China, Indonesia, South Africa, and former Eastern bloc countries, which are being updated bi-annually (OECD 2012b). However, the OECD provides no comprehensive time-series rates of assistance to producers of non-agricultural goods to compare with the PSEs, nor of what took place in those advanced economies during earlier decades. Data for these earlier decades from today's developed economies is needed in order to assess how various countries' policies evolved during stages of development similar to those of today's middle-income countries.

Also, almost no comparable time-series estimates had been generated for developing countries in the two decades following the seminal work of Krueger, Schiff, and Valdés (1988, 1991) until the release in 2008 of a new database of agricultural distortions by the World Bank (Anderson and Valenzuela 2008, updated and extended by Anderson and Nelgen 2013). This new data set complements and extends the OECD's PSE/CSEs and the Krueger, Schiff, and Valdés studies. It provides similar estimates for many other significant developing economies, and it also provides estimates of new and more-comprehensive policy indicators.

The World Bank's database

The new World Bank database covers 82 countries which together account for between 90 and 96 percent of the world's population, farmers, agricultural GDP, food consumption, poverty, and total GDP. The sample countries also account for more than 85 percent of agricultural production and employment in each of Africa, Asia, Latin America, and the transition-economies region of Europe and Central Asia, as well as for all of agricultural production and farm employment in OECD countries. Not all countries had annual data for the entire 1955–2011 period, but the average number of years covered is 45 per country.

Policy indicators are computed for 75 different farm products, with an average of almost 11 per country. This product coverage represents about 70 percent of the gross value of agricultural production in each of the focus countries and just under two thirds of global agricultural production, valued at undistorted prices over the period covered. Of the world's 30 most valuable agricultural products, the indicators cover 77 percent of global output (ranging from two thirds for livestock to three-quarters for oilseeds and tropical crops and five-sixths for grains and tubers). These products represent 85 percent of global agricultural exports. Such comprehensive coverage of countries, products, and years offers a reliable picture of long-term trends and fluctuations in policy indicators for individual countries and commodities, as well as for country-groups, regions, and the world as a whole.

This data set reveals distinct patterns of price distortions across countries and over time, as well as policy turning points. After defining the indicators, these patterns are summarized here under four headings: intersectoral distortion variation across countries; intrasectoral variation across farm products; year-to-year variations in rates of distortion; and policy-instrument choices.

Measures of price distortions

Typically, agricultural and non-agricultural trade measures (border taxes and protectionist Non-Tariff Barriers, or NTBs), together with multiple exchange rates, have distorted prices of food and other tradable products more commonly than have trade subsidies, direct domestic producer or consumer subsidies, or domestic taxes or quotas that alter product or input prices. However, in high-income countries, export subsidies grew in importance in the 1970s and 1980s and, since the 1980s, domestic support measures that (to varying extents) are decoupled from production decisions have begun to play a larger role. Furthermore, since the inception of the World Trade Organization (WTO) in 1995, most NTBs have been converted to tariffs. In many countries, however, those tariffs have been legally bound at well above applied rates, and are specific to the quantity traded rather than a percentage of the import or export price, so that such countries have been able to continue to vary the extent of their border restrictions as international prices or domestic supplies fluctuate from year to year.

To capture the extent of government intervention on farmer incentives and food consumer prices, a Nominal Rate of Assistance (NRA) and a consumer tax equivalent (CTE) are estimated. The NRA and CTE measure distortions imposed by governments that create a gap between current domestic producer or consumer price and the price that would exist under free markets. Under the "small-country" assumption, these rates are computed for each product as the percentage by which government policies have raised gross returns to farmers or consumer prices above what they would have been had the government not intervened (or the percentage by which government policies have lowered gross returns or consumer prices, if NRA<0 or CTE<0). The NRA includes the output-price-altering equivalent of any product-specific input subsidies or taxes. (The NRA and CTE differ from the OECD's PSE and CSE in that the latter are expressed as a percentage of the distorted rather than the undistorted price, and hence are typically smaller than the NRA or CTE and cannot exceed 100 percent; and the CSE has the opposite sign to the CTE.) The NRA and CTE are almost always very highly correlated and, with relatively small domestic subsidies and taxes, are almost identical.

A weighted-average NRA for all available products is derived using the values of production at undistorted prices as product weights. To this NRA for available (covered) products is added a "guesstimate" of the NRA for noncovered farm products (on average, about 30 percent of the total in value terms), along with an estimate of the NRA from non-product-specific forms of assistance to (or taxation of) farmers.

Since the 1980s, some high-income governments have also provided decoupled assistance to farmers. Because that support, in principle, does not distort resource allocation, its NRA has been computed separately and is not included for comparison with the NRAs for other sectors or for agriculture in developing countries. Each year, each covered farm commodity's industry is classified as either import-competing, as producing an exportable, or as producing a nontradable. The aggregate non-covered farm industry group is also subdivided into these three categories. This classification allows the generation each year of the weighted-average NRAs for exporting versus import-competing producers, to capture changes in the anti-trade bias that typically prevails.

Also reported is a production-weighted average NRA for non-agricultural tradables, so that this rate may be compared to the rate for agricultural tradables via the calculation of a Relative Rate of Assistance (RRA). The RRA recognizes that farmers are affected not just by prices of their own products but also by the incentives faced by non-agricultural producers bidding for the same mobile resources. That is, it is relative prices, and hence relative rates of government assistance, that affect incentives to producers. The RRA is defined in percentage terms as:

$$RRA=100\ [(100+NRAag^{t})/(100+NRAnonag^{t})-1]$$

where NRAagt and NRAnonagt are the percentage NRAs for the tradable parts of the agricultural (including non-covered) and non-agricultural sectors, respectively (Anderson et al. 2008). Note that if both of these sectors are equally assisted, the RRA is zero. This measure is useful since, if it is below (or above) zero, it provides an internationally comparable indication of the extent to which a country's sectoral policy regime has an anti- (or pro-) agricultural bias.

The cost of government policy distortions in terms of resource misallocation tends to be greater as the degree of substitution in production or consumption increases. In the case of food, which involves the use of land that is sector-specific but transferrable among farm activities, the greater the dispersion of NRAs across industries within the sector, the higher will be the welfare cost of those market interventions. For that reason it is also useful to draw on indicators developed by Anderson and Neary (2005) and adapted for agriculture by Lloyd, Croser, and Anderson (2010). These are a Welfare Reduction Index (WRI) and a Trade Reduction Index (TRI). The former measure recognizes that the welfare cost of a price distortion imposed by a government is related to the square of the price wedge and thus is positive, regardless of whether the government's policy favors or hurts producers or consumers in a particular sector. The TRI measures the extent to which import protection or export taxation reduces the volume of trade. It is the percentage uniform trade tax which, if applied equally to all agricultural tradables, would generate the same reduction in trade volume as the actual intra-sectoral structure of distortions to domestic prices of such tradable goods. Similarly, the WRI is the percentage uniform trade tax which, if applied equally to all agricultural tradables, would generate the same reduction in national economic welfare as the actual intra-sectoral structure of distortions to domestic prices of these tradable goods.

Impacts of Policies on Domestic Food and Agricultural Prices

We begin with indicators of trends in inter-sectoral distortions to producer incentives, then examine trends in intra-sectoral distortions to food and agricultural prices, before turning to year-to-year fluctuations around the trend indicators and then the contribution of various policy instruments to those indicators.

Variations in inter-sectoral distortions

Historically, the higher a country's per capita income, the higher have tended to be its nominal—and especially relative—rates of assistance to agriculture (NRAs and RRAs) and its food CTEs. More generally, policy regimes, on average, have had a pro-agricultural bias in high-income countries and an anti-agricultural bias in developing countries, and an anti-food consumer bias in high-income countries and a pro-food consumer bias in developing countries. However, since the 1980s, these biases have diminished, and the two groups' average RRAs have converged toward zero (Figures 1 and 2). So too have their CTEs.

In the case of developing countries, it is clear from Figure 2(a) that the rise in their average RRA is due as much to a decline in assistance to nonfarm sectors (especially cuts to manufacturing protection) as to declines in agricultural disincentives (especially cuts to export taxes). However, the extent and speed of convergence vary across regions. Among developing countries, convergence has been greatest for Asia and least for Africa; among high-income countries, it has been greatest for the European Union and almost non-existent for other Western European countries (non-EU WE). The sole exception is the dip for most countries in 2005–10, when international food prices rose steeply. For EU members, the RRA declined from an average of 77 percent in the 1980s to 11 percent in 2005–10.

As a consequence of the changes in NRAs and CTEs, the trade- and welfare-reduction indexes of the two main country-groups have traced an inverted-U shape, rising to the mid-1980s before more than halving since then (Figure 3).

The averages reported in Figures 1–3 hide the fact that both the level and rate of change in distortion indicators still vary considerably across countries. National RRA estimates for 2005–09 varied from around −40 percent for several African countries to around 100 percent for a few high-income countries (Figure 4). Clearly, much could be gained from further reforms to remove these cross-country differences, which would lead to international relocations of production and consumption.

The extent to which RRAs vary at any level of per capita income or comparative advantage is substantial. Based on regression analysis over the time series from 1955 to 2007, per capita income and comparative advantage account for 59 percent of the variation in RRAs globally. Note that the average RRA for developing countries, which converged toward zero from the 1980s, did not stop at zero, but rather "overshot". For Korea and Taiwan, this evolution to a positive RRA occurred in the early 1970s, for the Philippines it happened in the later 1980s, and for China, India, Indonesia, and Malaysia it happened in the first decade of the current century. By just focusing on agricultural NRAs, and bearing in mind the sharp rise in international prices of farm products in 2008, it is clear from Figure 5 that agricultural protection is growing in Asia's three most-populous countries.

Variations in intra-sectoral distortions

Within a country's agricultural sector, whether the country is developed or developing, product NRAs vary widely (Figure 6). Some commodity product NRAs are positive and high in almost all countries (sugar, rice, and milk). Others are positive and high in developed economies but highly negative in developing countries (most noticeably, cotton). Still other product NRAs are relatively low in all countries (feed grains and soybeans as inputs into intensive livestock; pork and poultry as standard-technology industrial activities).

The failure of global variability across commodities to decrease signifi-

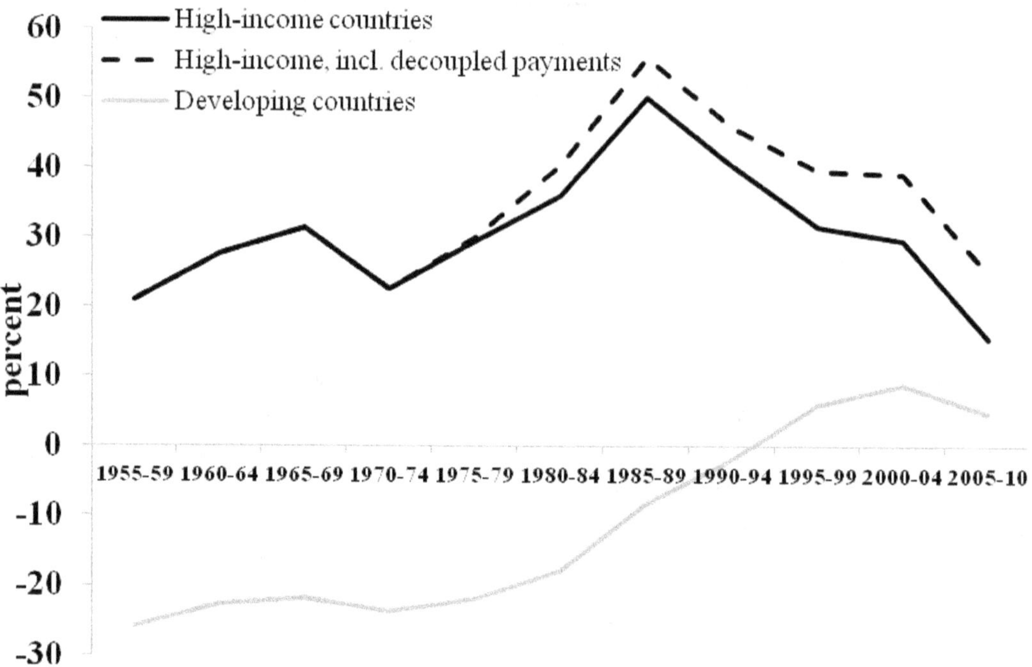

Figure 1. NRAs to agriculture in high-income (HIC), transition (ECA),[a] and developing countries, 1955–2010 (%). Five-year weighted averages with decoupled payments included in the dashed line.

[a] ECA is a term used by the World Bank to denote the transitional economies of Central and Eastern Europe and Central Asia.

Source: Anderson (2009, Chapter 1), updated from estimates in Anderson and Nelgen (2013)

(a)

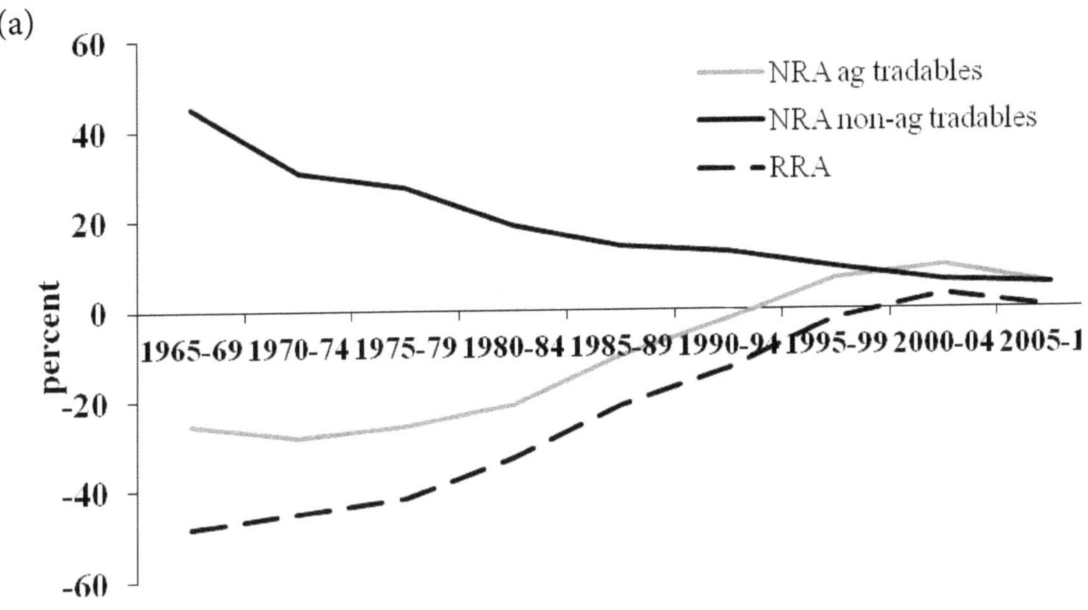

(b)

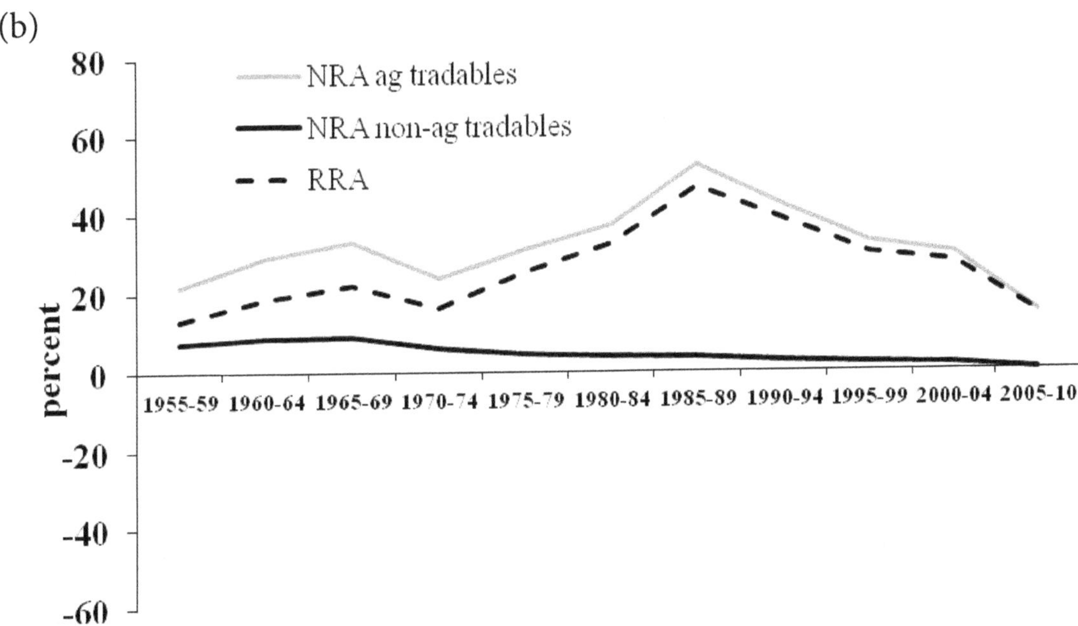

Figure 2. (a) Developing and (b) high-income countries' NRAs to agricultural and non-agricultural tradable sectors, and RRAs, 1955–2010 (%). Calculations use farm production-weighted averages across countries. RRA is defined as $100[(100+NRAag^t)/(100+NRAnonag^t)-1]$, where $NRAag^t$ and $NRAnonag^t$, respectively, are the percentage NRAs for the tradable segments of the agricultural and non-agricultural sectors.

Source: Anderson (2009, Chapter 1), updated from estimates in Anderson and Nelgen (2013)

(a)

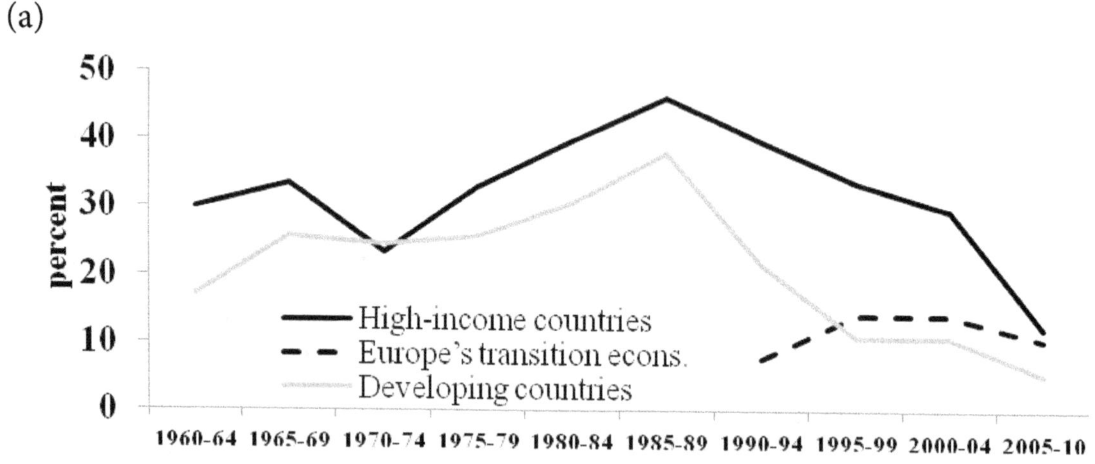

(b)

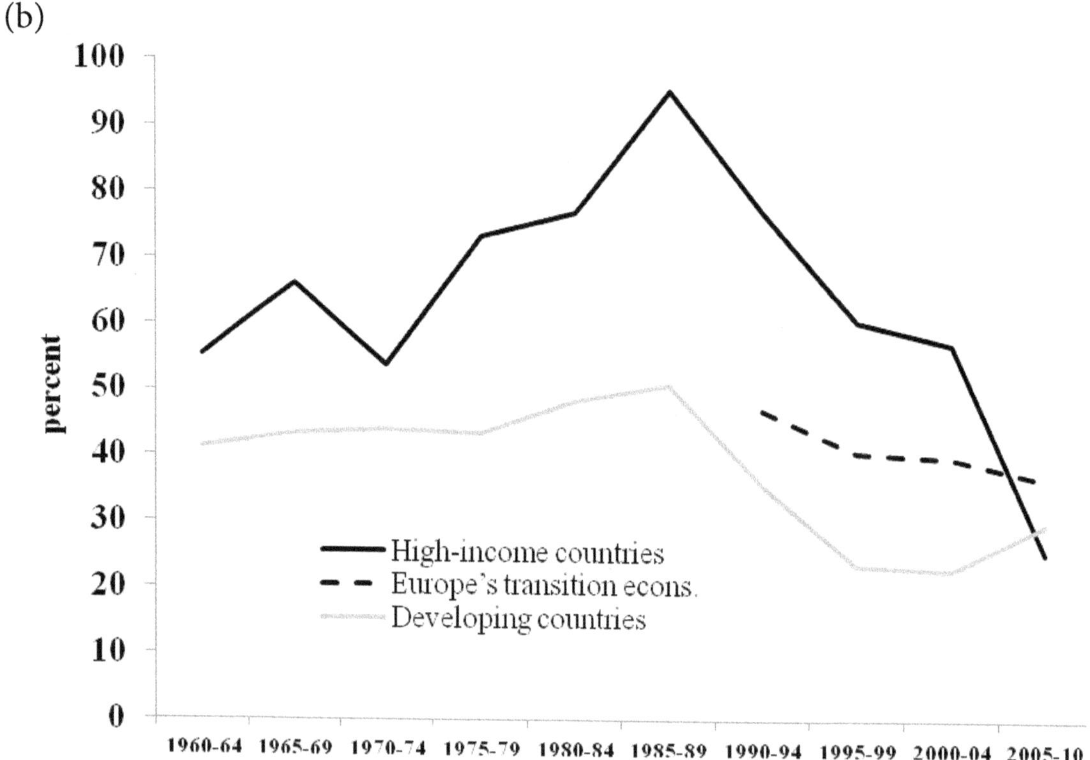

Figure 3. (a) Trade-reduction index (TRI) and (b) welfare-reduction index (WRI) among high-income, transition, and developing countries for tradable farm products, 1960–2010 (%).

Source: Lloyd, Croser, and Anderson (2010), based on time-series estimates in Anderson and Croser (2009), and updated using Anderson and Nelgen (2013)

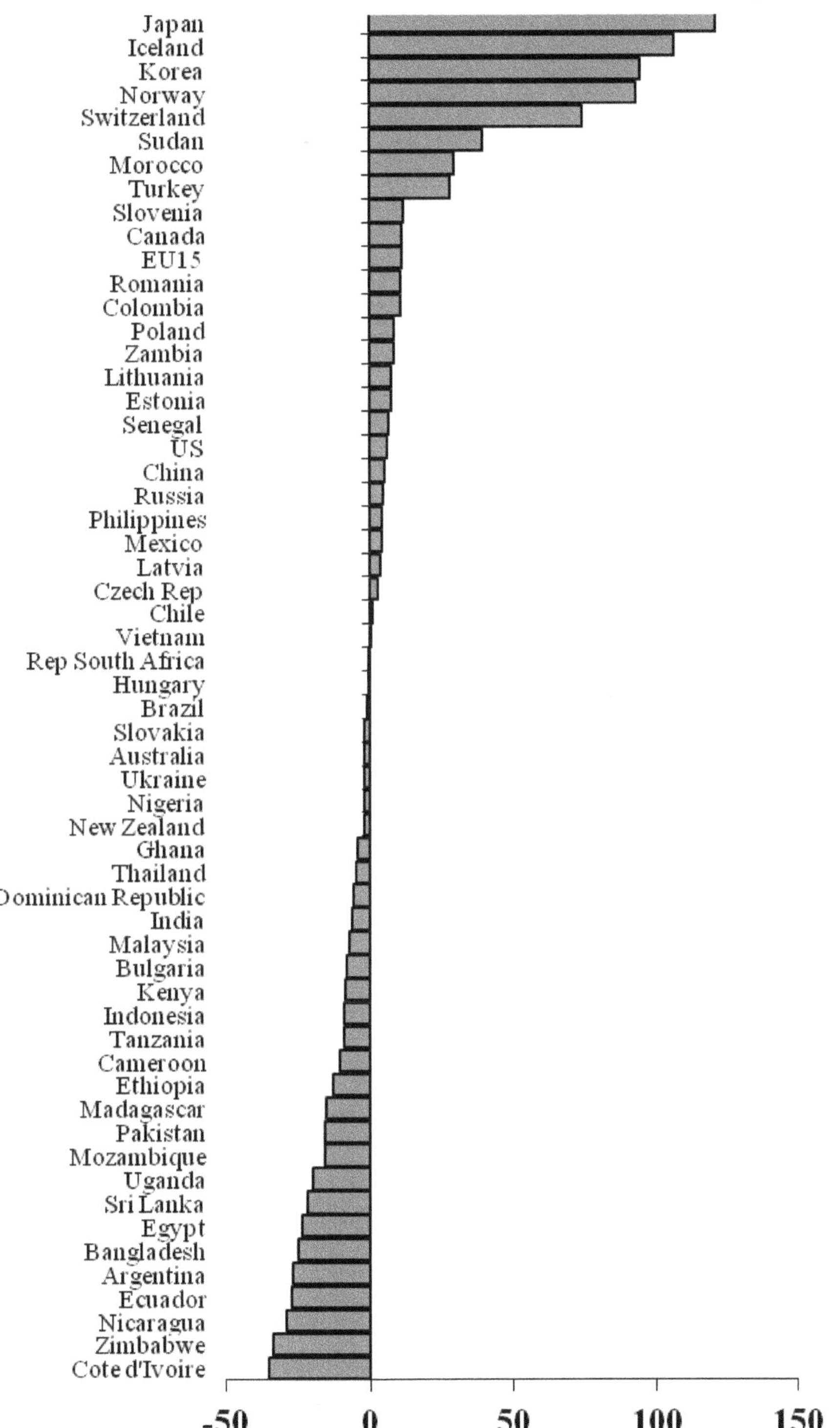

Figure 4. RRAs by country, 2005–10.
Source: Updated from Anderson (2009, Chapter 1), using Anderson and Nelgen (2013)

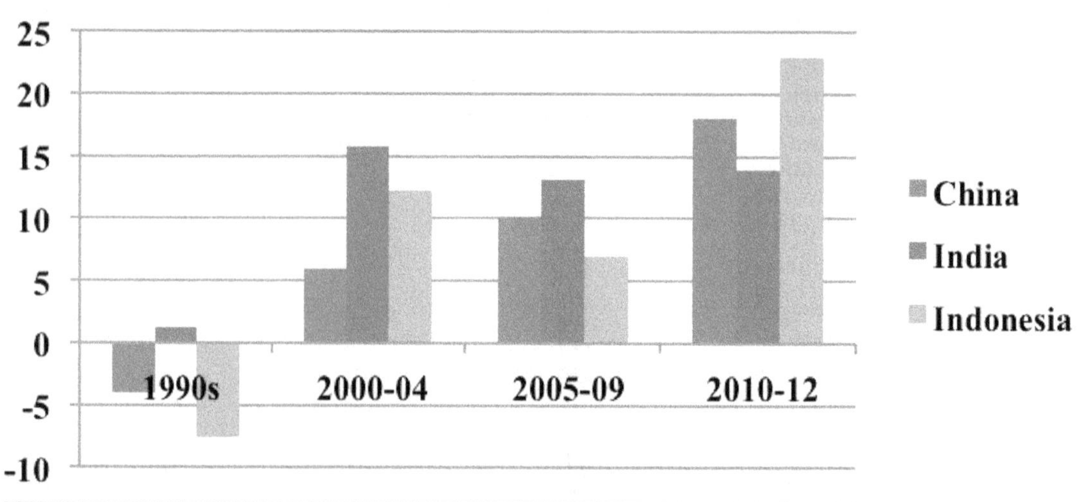

Figure 5. Agricultural NRAs in China, India, and Indonesia, 1990 to 2012 (%).
Source: Compiled from estimates in Anderson and Nelgen (2013)
Note: For India the final bar refers only to 2010.

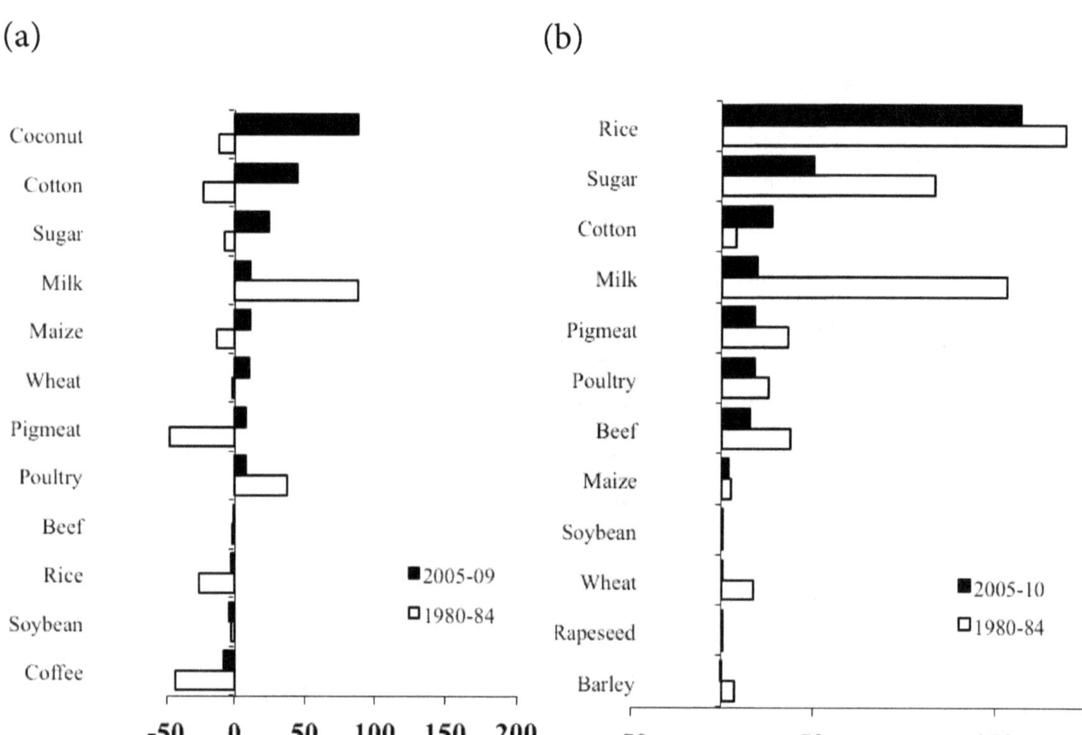

Figure 6. Comparison of earlier (1980–84) and more recent (2005–10) NRAs in (a) developing and (b) high-income countries, by product (%).

cantly suggests that the movement of the mean-NRA toward zero has not been accompanied by a fall in the variance across commodities within the sector. This pattern explains why the WRI in Figure 3(b) is still well above zero, since the welfare cost of a sector's policy regime is greater the more dispersed are commodity NRAs within that sector. As is the case for variations in sectoral distortion across countries, much could be gained from intra-country resource re-allocation within the agricultural sector and from the altered consumption patterns that would emerge from removing cross-product differences in NRAs.

A crucial component of the NRAs' product dispersion is that the agricultural-policy regimes across countries tend to have an anti-trade bias. This bias has declined over time for the developing-country group, mainly owing to declines in agricultural-export taxation, and despite growing agricultural-import protection. For the high-income group, agricultural export subsidies rose to the mid-1980s and then declined, as did import protection (Figure 7). These factors explain the smaller decline in the TRI for high-income versus developing countries shown in Figure 3(a).

Year-to-year fluctuations around the trend level of distortions

Around the long-run trend for each country there has been much fluctuation from year to year in individual product NRAs (and CTEs, not shown here because they are almost the same at the aggregate level). This tendency has not diminished since the mid-1980s for developing countries, and it has even increased for high-income countries. The negative correlation of a commodity's NRA with movements in its international price is largely responsible for this pattern. On average, barely half of the change in an international price is transmitted to domestic markets within the first year. As noted earlier, governments are keen to prevent domestic prices from being affected by spikes in international prices. In both agricultural-exporting and agricultural-importing countries, and in high-income as well as in developing countries, large changes in NRAs and CTEs occur during periods of international price spikes—whether up, as in 1974 and 2008, or down, as in 1986 (Anderson and Nelgen 2012). One manifestation of that is clear in Figure 8, which shows for each of rice and wheat the strong negative correlation between the international price and the NRA—even when averaged across all countries.

Contributions of various policy instruments to distortion indicators

Across countries and time periods, governments have used a broad array of policy instruments. They include distortions to input markets (largely subsidies, plus controls on land use), production quotas, marketing quotas, target prices, price subsidies or taxes in output markets, and especially, border measures that directly tax, subsidize, or quantitatively restrict international trade. The major vehicles responsible for the losses associated with those distortions are trade policy instruments such as export and import taxes and subsidies or quantitative restrictions, along with (in the past) multiple exchange rates. These trade policy instruments account for no less than three-fifths of agricultural NRAs globally. As a result, they are responsible for an even larger share of the global welfare cost and agricultural WRIs, since trade measures also tax consumers, and welfare costs are proportional to the

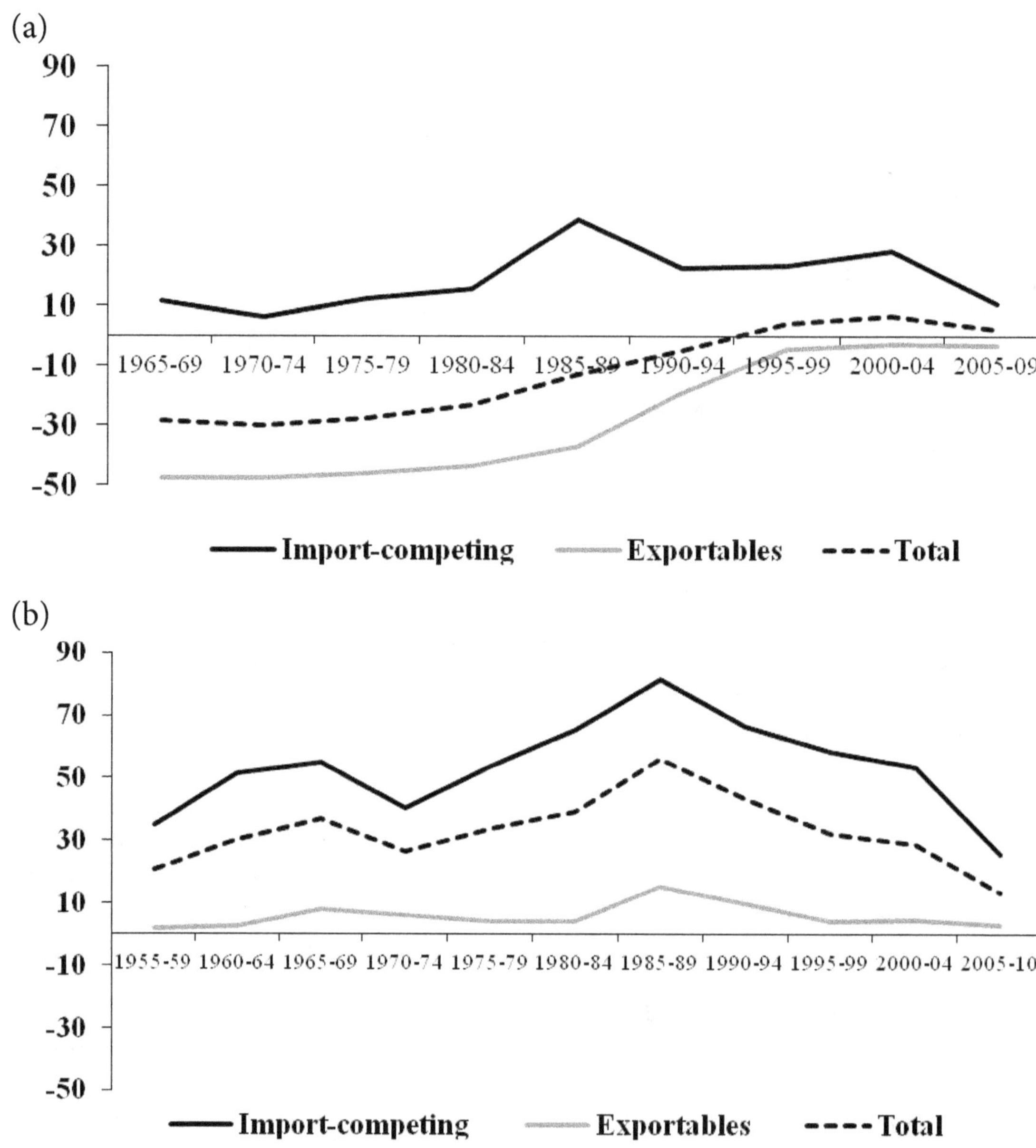

Figure 7. NRAs to exportable, import-competing, and all covered agricultural products in (a) developing and (b) high-income and European transition economies, 1955–2010 (%). Five-year weighted averages for covered products only. The total also includes nontradables. The straight line in the upper segment of each graph represents an ordinary-least-squares regression based on annual NRA estimates.
Source: Anderson (2009, Chapter 1), updated using Anderson and Nelgen (2013)

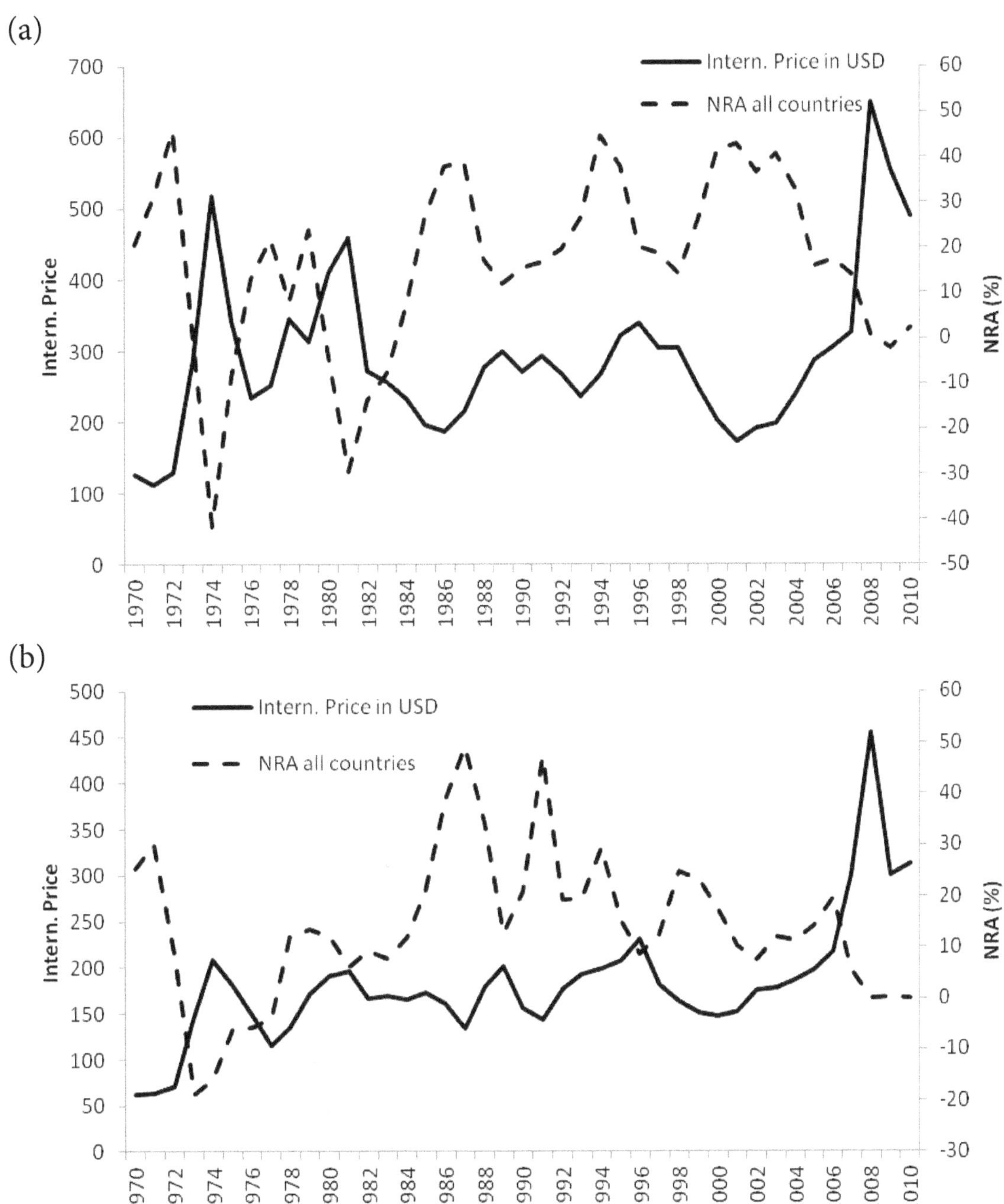

Figure 8: (a) Rice and (b) wheat NRAs and their international price, 82 countries, 1970 to 2011 (left axis is international price in current US$, right axis is weighted average NRA in percent).
Source: Based on the NRA estimates in Anderson and Nelgen (2013)

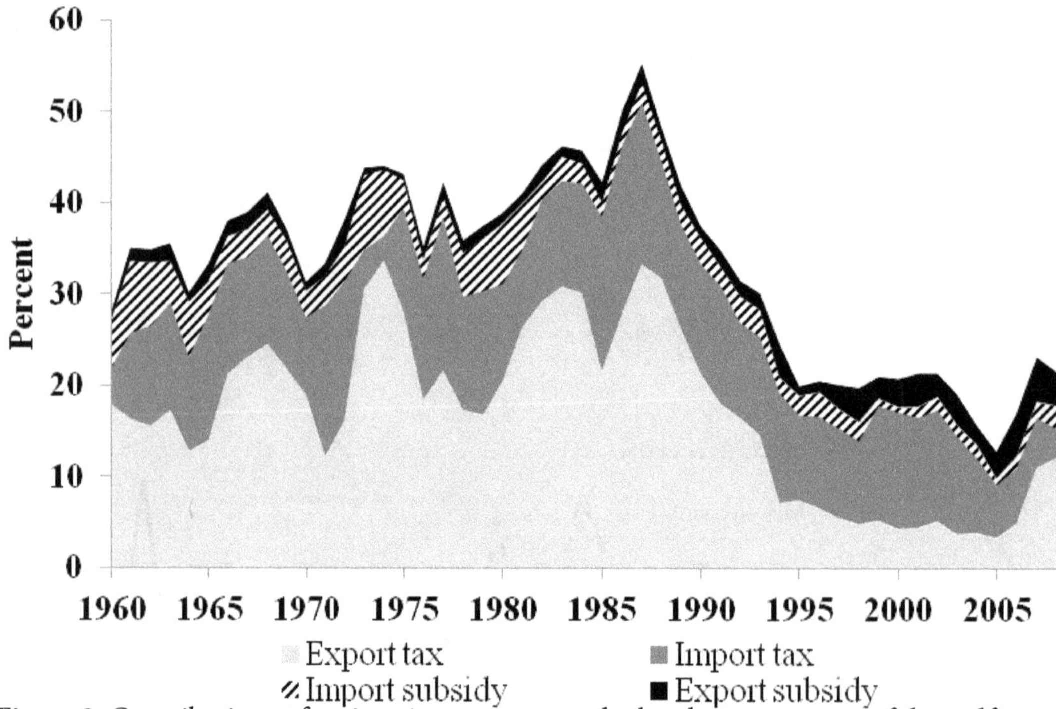

Figure 9. Contributions of various instruments to the border component of the welfare reduction index (WRI) for developing countries, 1960–2010 (%).

Source: Derived from estimates reported in Croser and Anderson (2011), updated using Anderson and Nelgen (2013)

square of a trade tax. In contrast, internal domestic agricultural policies that directly subsidize or tax outputs and inputs have contributed only minimally to NRAs in the past, and little or nothing to food CTEs.

Among trade-distorting policy instruments, it is clear from Figure 9 how much export taxes have been phased out by developing countries. In sharp contrast, as assistance to import-competing agricultural sub-sectors of developing countries has grown (Figure 6(a)), the relative importance (from a national welfare perspective) of import taxes has increased dramatically (Figure 9). In Western Europe, the growth of decoupled, more-direct income-support measures, along with the virtual abolition of all support measures in Australia and New Zealand, reveals a far different pattern than in high-income countries in East Asia, where border-measure supports continue to dominate (Figure 10).

Input subsidies are a relatively minor component of most countries' assistance to farmers. But they lingered on in Australia and New Zealand when most other forms of assistance were being phased out, and such subsidies have also remained about one-fifth of the total NRA in the United States (Anderson 2009, Chapters 4 and 5). With two notable exceptions, input subsidies are even less common in developing countries, where funds for such direct subsidies are scarcer. The important exceptions are India and Indonesia. In India, input subsidies contributed 7 to 9 percentage points to the agricultural NRA in the 1990s and 10 points in 2000–04. In Indonesia, such subsidies have contributed 2 to 4 percentage points to the agricultural NRA since 1990. They also contributed from 5 to 9 points in the 1970s and 1980s, even at times when the overall agricultural sector of those countries had a negative NRA.

Up to the 1980s—and in some cases the early 1990s—it was quite common for developing-country governments to intervene in the market for foreign exchange. Such interventions added to the anti-trade biases that were targeted at tradable sectors, including agriculture. However, these interventions largely disappeared by the mid-1990s, as part of reforms to macroeconomic policy. In China, for example, trade taxation associated with the country's dual-exchange-rate system accounted for almost one-fifth of its (negative) RRA in the 1980s. However, since the mid-1990s, that system has been abolished (Huang et al. 2009).

As governments seek to prevent domestic prices from being affected by periodic spikes in international prices, large changes in the relative importance of different policy instruments occur. This is evident from the estimated contributions to total agricultural WRIs of various policy instruments during the upward price spikes around 1974 and 2008 and the downward spike around 1986 (Figure 9). In some cases, trade taxes even temporarily disappeared; in other cases, trade subsidies emerged or expanded. Even when aggregated over all developing countries, the contribution of export taxes and import subsidies to the overall WRI rises and falls with international prices, while the opposite is true of import taxes and export subsidies.

Summary of global transfers from/to farmers and food consumers

How have the net implicit transfers from or to producers and consumers altered as a result of the reforms begun in the 1980s? There has been a dramatic change in the proportions of the global farm population facing negative versus positive NRAs, and in the proportions of the global value (at undistorted prices) of agri-

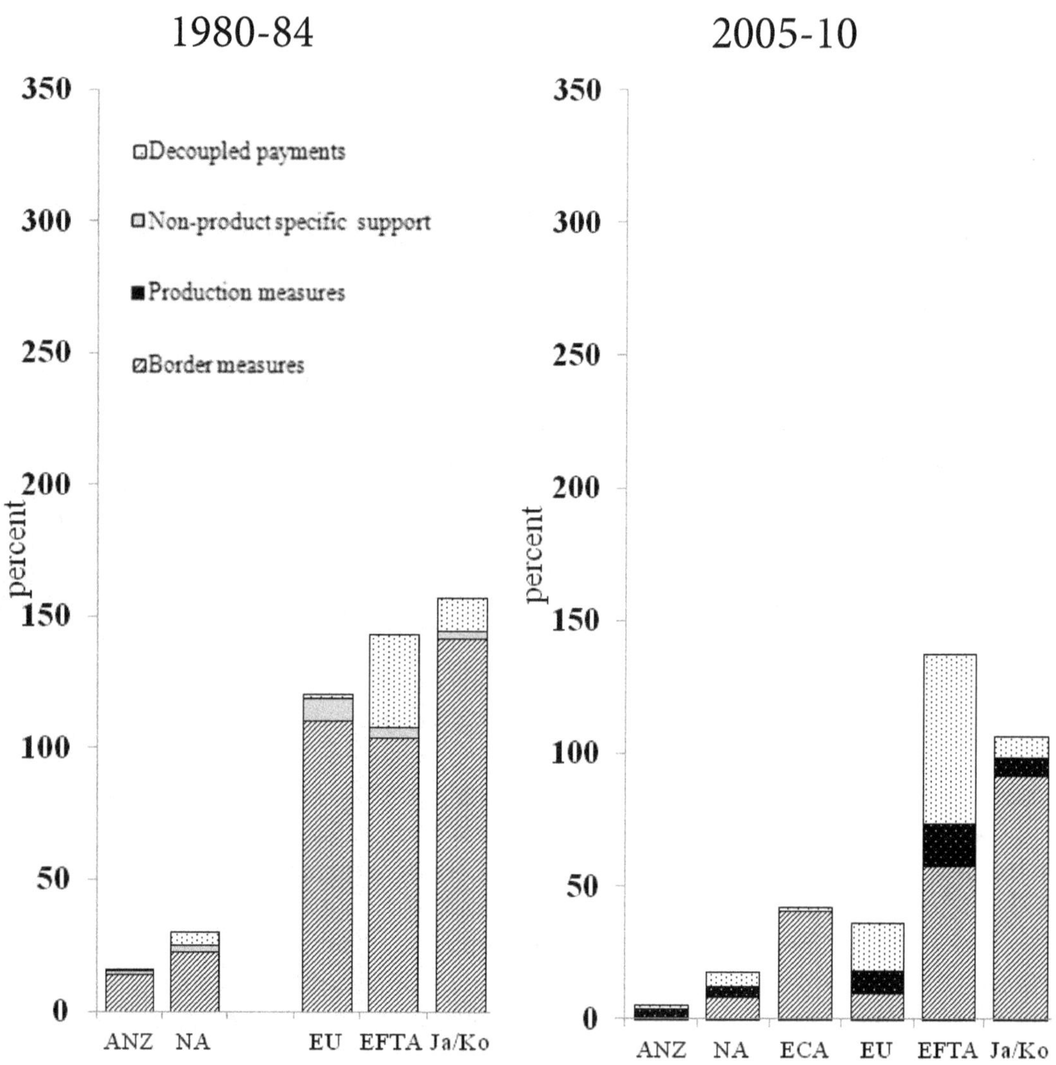

Figure 10: Comparison of earlier (1980–84) and more recent (2005–10) contributions of various policy instruments to the producer component of the welfare reduction index (WRI) for selected high-income and transition countries (%).

Source: Croser and Anderson (2011), updated using Anderson and Nelgen (2013)

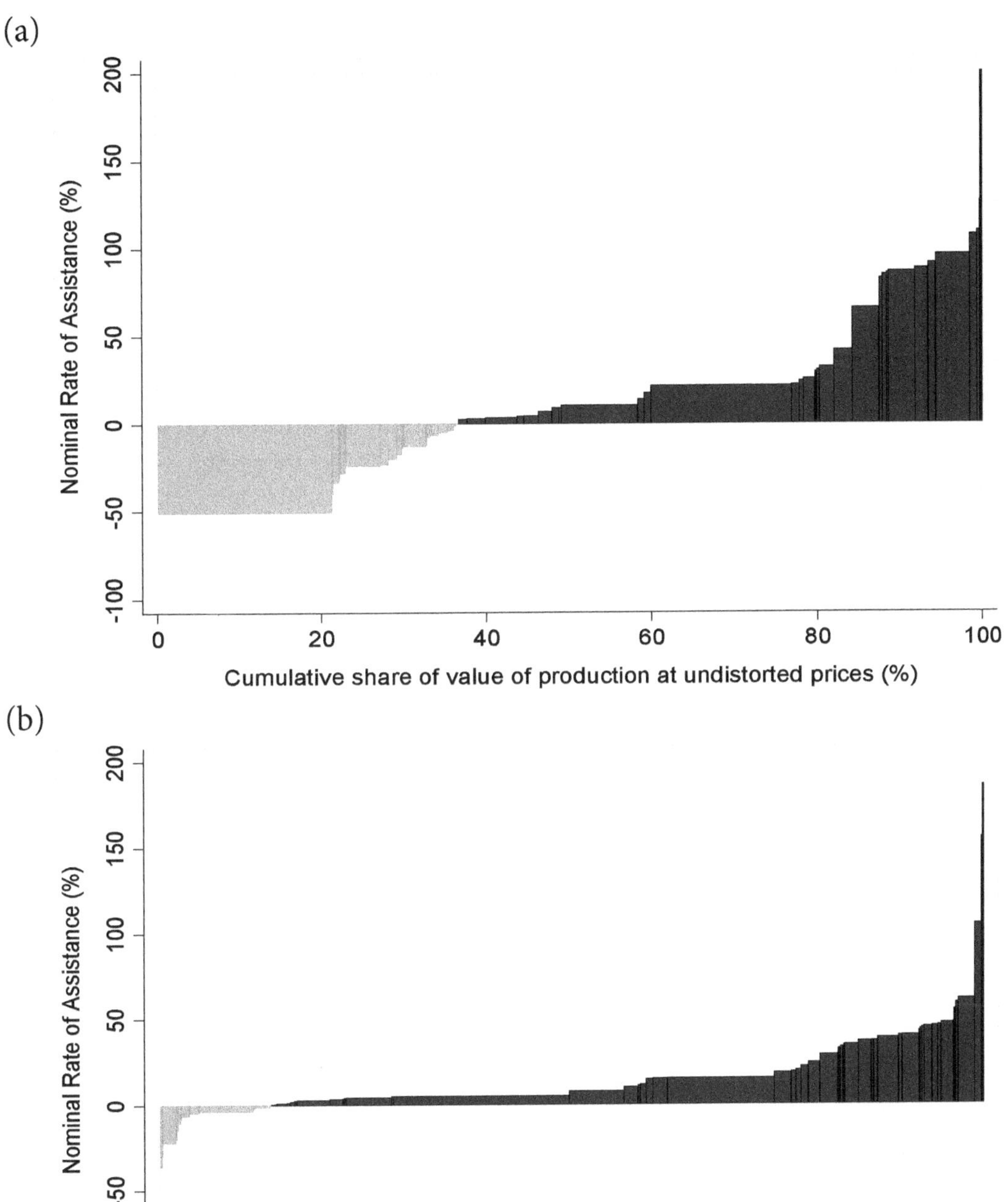

Figure 11: Proportions of the global value (at undistorted prices) of agricultural production facing various NRAs: (a) 1980–89a (grey = –\$83 billion, black = \$182 billion, so global net is \$99 billion) and (b) 2000–09 (grey = –\$15 billion, black = \$313 billion, so global net is \$298 billion).

[a] Iceland (299%), Switzerland (290%), and Norway (213%) are shown as just 200%, so as to fit on page.

Source: Generated by Signe Nelgen from estimates in Anderson and Nelgen (2013).

cultural production facing various NRAs. This is illustrated in Figure 11. The global data underlying that figure involve a transfer from farmers to consumers or governments of $83 billion and from consumers or governments to farmers of $182 billion per year in the 1980s, hence an annual net transfer to farmers of $99 billion globally. By the 2000s, however, the annual transfer from farmers had diminished greatly such that the net transfer to farmers had trebled to $298 billion globally—despite the reduced rate of support for farmers in high-income countries. Associated with those policy reforms are reductions in the distortions to consumer prices of food products. Since the 1980s the aggregate global transfer to food consumers has shrunk considerably, but so too has the aggregate global transfer from food consumers. This is depicted in Figure 12, which shows the proportion of the global non-farm population facing various levels of food consumer taxes or subsidies.

Food Policy Going Forward: What Prospect for Further Reform?

From the above evidence it is clear that there is now room for some optimism about the prospects for future food and agricultural policy reform. Admittedly, it is troubling that some developing countries have moved from negative to positive RRAs and that agricultural protection has recently increased in three of the most important developing countries, namely China, India, and Indonesia. In high-income countries, too, although the indicators reveal declining NRAs, these trends do not necessarily reflect actual policy changes but rather incomplete transmission of higher international food prices in the past five years. Even so, many countries' RRAs do appear to have converged toward zero, and in numerous high-income countries there has been a move away from the most-distorting policy instruments (trade measures) to measures that are somewhat de-coupled from production and often completely de-coupled from consumption. Global and regional institutions have played an important role in contributing to those reforms. Of particular importance to the decline in price distortions in the European Union has been the General Agreement on Tariffs and Trade, via the Uruguay Round agreements that are now incorporated in the World Trade Organization (Swinnen 2008).

However, the recently ramped-up biofuel subsidies and renewable energy mandates in the United States and European Union (which are not captured in the indictors reported above) are putting upward pressure on the trend level and possibly variance of international food prices—in contrast to traditional agricultural policies which historically have depressed those prices. Might this become the new agricultural protection in high-income countries? Or might groups concerned with global food security be successful (possibly in collaboration with environmentalists if/when they become convinced that this type of renewable energy is not a net benefit to the environment) in persuading governments to abandon their biofuel support policies? As for the recent growth of agricultural protection in rapidly emerging economies, hopefully greater transparency and heightened scrutiny of new policy developments by the OECD Secretariat and others will provide enough counter-pressure in national polities to offset the inevitable lobbying pressure from farmers and agribusiness.

References

Anderson, J.E., and J.P. Neary. 2005. *Measuring the Restrictiveness of International Trade Policy.* Cambridge, MA: MIT Press.

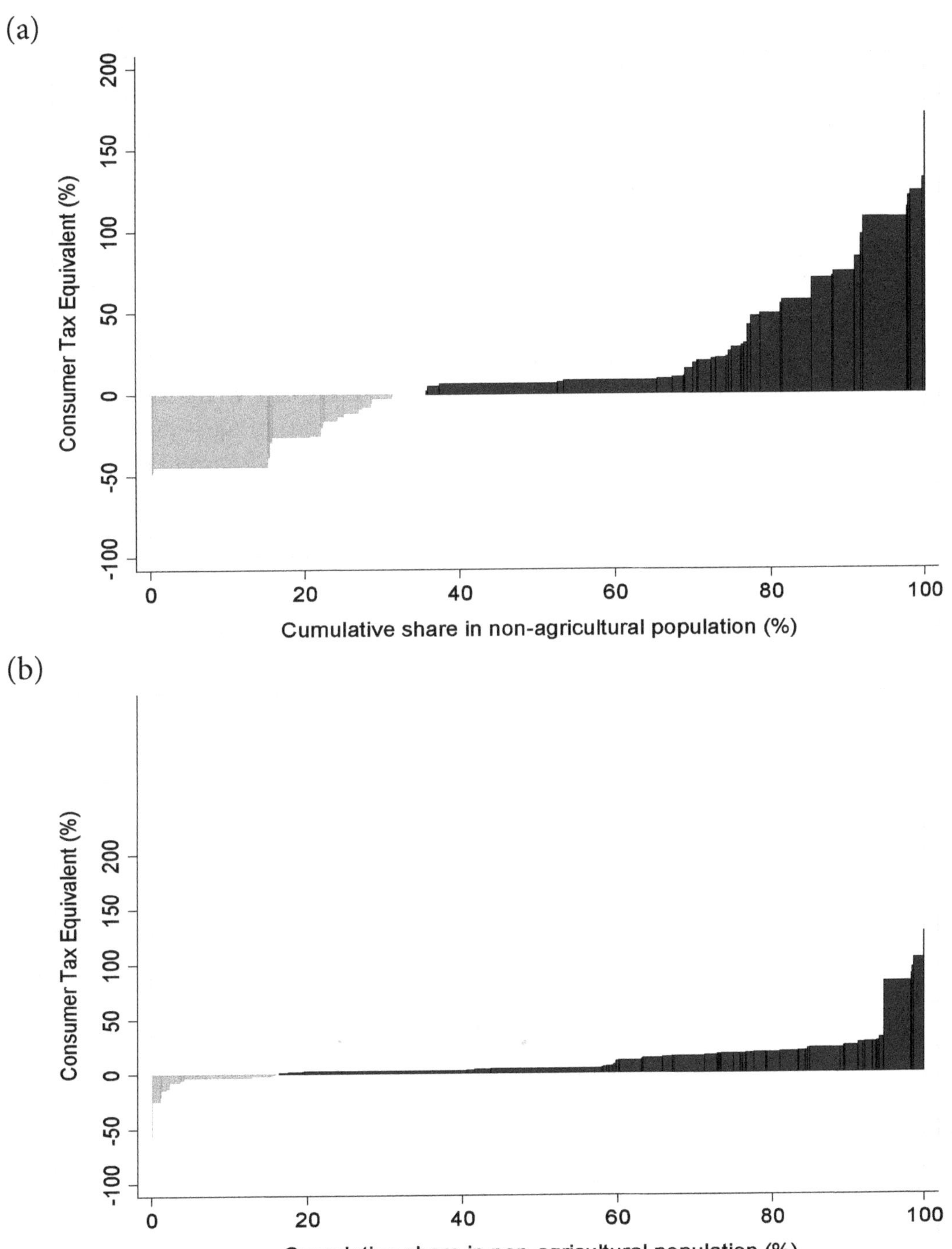

Figure 12: Proportions of global non-farm population facing various consumer tax equivalents on their purchases of farm products, (a) 1980–89 and (b) 2000–09
Source: Generated by Signe Nelgen from estimates in Anderson and Nelgen (2013).

Anderson, K., ed. 2009. *Distortions to Agricultural Incentives: A Global Perspective, 1955–2007*. London: Palgrave Macmillan and Washington, DC: The World Bank.

Anderson, K., and E. Valenzuela. 2008. *Estimates of Distortions to Agricultural Incentives, 1955 to 2007*. Database spreadsheets at www.worldbank.org/agdistortions.

Anderson, K., G. Rausser, and J.F.M. Swinnen. 2013. "Political Economy of Public Policies: Insights from Distortions to Agricultural and Food Markets." *Journal of Economic Literature* 51 (2): 423-77.

Anderson, K., J. Cockburn, and W. Martin, eds. 2010. *Agricultural Price Distortions, Inequality, and Poverty*. Washington, DC: The World Bank.

Anderson, K., and J.L. Croser. 2009. *National and Global Agricultural Trade and Welfare Reduction Indexes, 1955 to 2007*. Spreadsheet at www.worldbank.org/agdistortions.

Anderson, K., M. Kurzweil, W. Martin, D. Sandri, and E. Valenzuela. 2008. "Measuring Distortions to Agricultural Incentives, Revisited." *World Trade Review* 7 (4): 675-704.

Anderson, K., and S. Nelgen. 2012. "Trade Barrier Volatility and Agricultural Price Stabilization." *World Development* 40 (1): 36-48.

Anderson, K., and S. Nelgen. 2013. *Updated National and Global Estimates of Distortions to Agricultural Incentives, 1955 to 2011*. Database spreadsheets at www.worldbank.org/agdistortions.

Carter, C.A., G.C. Rausser, and A. Smith. 2011. "Commodity Booms and Busts." *Annual Review of Resource Economics*, 3: 87–118.

Croser, J.L., and K. Anderson. 2011. "Changing Contributions of Different Agricultural Policy Instruments to Global Reductions in Trade and Welfare." *World Trade Review* 10 (3): 297-323.

Huang, J., S. Rozelle, W. Martin, and Y. Liu. 2009. "Distortions to Agricultural Incentives in China." In *Distortions to Agricultural Incentives in Asia*, edited by K. Anderson, and W. Martin, 117-61. Washington, DC: The World Bank.

Krueger, A.O., M. Schiff, and A. Valdés. 1988. "Agricultural Incentives in Developing Countries." *World Bank Economic Review* 2 (3): 255-72.

Krueger, A.O., M. Schiff, and A. Valdés. 1991. *The Political Economy of Agricultural Pricing Policy. Vol. 1, Latin America; Vol. 2, Asia; and Vol. 3, Africa and the Mediterranean*. Baltimore: Johns Hopkins University Press for the World Bank.

Lloyd, P.J., J.L. Croser, and K. Anderson. 2010. "Global Distortions to Agricultural Markets: New Indicators of Trade and Welfare Impacts, 1960 to 2007." *Review of Development Economics* 14 (2): 141-60.

Martin, W., and K. Anderson. 2012. "Export Restrictions and Price Insulation during Commodity Price Booms." *American Journal of Agricultural Economics* 94 (2): 422-27.

OECD. 2012a. *Producer and Consumer Support Estimates Database*. http://www.oecd.org (for 1986–2011).

OECD. 2012b. *Agricultural Policy Monitoring and Evaluation 2011: OECD Countries and Emerging Economies*. Paris: Organisation for Economic Co-operation and Development.

Swinnen, J.F.M., ed. 2008. *The Perfect Storm: The Political Economy of the Fischler Reforms of the Common Agricultural Policy.* Brussels: Centre for European Policy Studies.

World Food System Disruptions in the Early 2000s: Causes, Impacts, and Cures

Joachim von Braun[1], Bernardina Algieri[2], Matthias Kalkuhl[3]

The rapidly rising and more-volatile food prices of recent years are a significant indication of changes in global markets and a signal of resource scarcity. They pose new challenges in terms of food and nutrition security at the worldwide level. This article traces the main drivers and impacts of food price increases, and proposes institutional changes in the world food system to help overcome chronic supply constraints through enhanced productivity, combined with actions to address new causes of food price volatility, such as financialization of commodity markets and linkages to energy markets. The price crises of 2008 and 2011, and to a lesser extent in 2012, have been met with often, uncoordinated national policy adjustments with international implications. To prevent such collective actions failures in the international food system, comprehensive institutional changes are proposed.

Keywords: price volatility, price crises, food security, governance

JEL Classification: F55, O19, Q02, Q18

Introduction

The spikes in food prices over the last six years and their extreme volatility, i.e., unpredictable and large swings in prices, are an expression of changes in global markets and a signal of resource scarcity. Briefly interrupted only in the mid-1970s, international real food prices recorded a declining trend that lasted for decades. Prices then stabilized around a slightly increasing trend for five to six years until mid-2007, when they started a sharp rise, reaching a twin peak first in June/July 2008 and then in December 2010/January 2011. Since then, international real prices have been volatile, with several peaks and troughs.

The breaking of the long-term price decline experienced since 2008 and the extreme volatility of food prices present major challenges for the world's policymakers, who are increasingly faced with rising food insecurity, combined with political and economic risks, like social unrests, and accelerated inflation. Lack of predictability and uncertainty associated with increased volatility hampers economic growth in poor countries (Jacks, O'Rourke, and Williamson 2011), undermines progress in nutritional status and peoples' food security (FAO 2011), and amplifies the incidence of poverty, when the real income of the poor declines (Benson et al. 2013; Ivanic and Martin 2008). Furthermore, price volatility may complicate environmental management for commodity-dependent countries and financial planning, since companies tend to postpone investment expenditures when they experience increased uncertainty concerning future commodity prices (Ferderer 1997).

[1] Corresponding author, Professor for Economic and Technological Change, Director, Center for Development Research, University of Bonn, Germany. www.zef.de.

[2] Lecturer, University of Calabria, Italy.

[3] Senior Researcher, Center for Development Research, University of Bonn, Germany.

In this context, the present study aims to examine in greater detail the causes of sustained increases in agricultural prices and price volatility in order to assess the emerging risks for developing countries and to propose a set of institutional changes in the world food system to overcome the risks of extreme booms and busts in food prices. It outlines potential approaches for coping with chronic supply constraints through enhanced productivity and suggests actions connected to the new drivers of food crises, linked to financial markets, energy, water, and climate change. Effective remedies will require a combination of new public-policy actions that foster agricultural growth and protect the vulnerable. Finally, the paper reviews several promising international initiatives carried out recently by the private sector to stabilize prices. The remainder of the paper is organized as follows: the second section investigates the main determinants of high and volatile food prices, and groups them into three main categories: fundamentals, macro-factors, and new drivers; the third section analyses the core consequences brought about by high prices and volatility; and the fourth section presents a set of policy actions to be pursued in order to curb extreme price rises and volatility, and mitigate the negative effects on the most vulnerable.

An overview of the main causes of price hikes and volatility

After remaining at historically low levels for decades, food prices started rising and becoming more volatile in the mid-2000s. In 2007–2008, the price of almost every food item sharply increased. At their peaks in the second quarter of 2008, world prices of wheat and maize were three times higher than at the beginning of 2003, and the price of rice was five times higher (Figure 1). Prices dropped thereafter, mainly because food demand slowed with the global financial crisis and recession; they spiked again in 2011 and in the third quarter of 2012.

At a more aggregated level and in real terms, the Food and Agriculture Organization's (FAO) food-price index, tracking important international food commodity prices, as well as the FAO's cereals price index which includes grains and rice replicate the price movements of the four staple crops (Figure 2). Although the FAO indices use weights based on export volumes which do not mirror the diet composition of the poor in developing countries, they give a first proxy of the magnitude of food price changes.

The fact that agricultural commodities, especially cereals, experienced three significant price spikes in about six years suggests that something serious is shaking the world's food chain. Determinants of high prices and volatility are complex and numerous, and they include traditional agricultural fundamentals as well as macro-economic factors. Additionally, they involve new determinants linked to energy and worldwide financial markets. Figure 3 provides a synthesis of the different drivers which will be discussed in more detail below.

Market fundamentals that led to price increases operate via demand and supply channels, and include greater costs of production due to higher energy and fertilizer prices, high demand coming mainly from emerging markets, primarily China and India, and general fluctuations in harvests (Abbott, Hurt, and Tyner 2008; 2011; Trostle 2008). The inelastic nature of food demand and supply exacerbates shocks as production can only respond slowly to in-

Figure 1. International grain prices

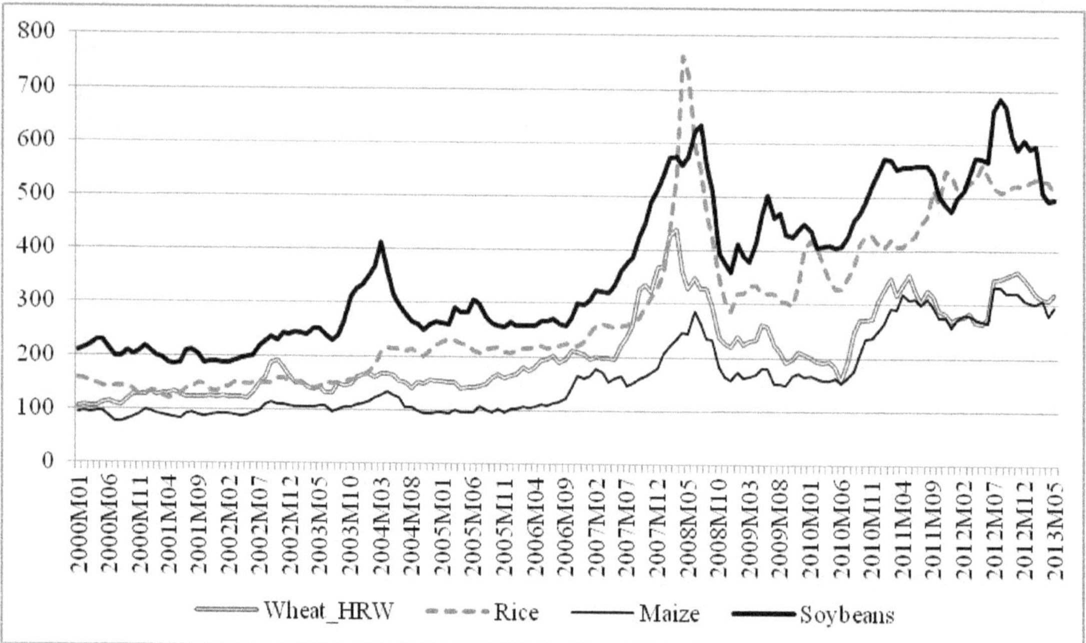

Note: y-axis: $/metric tons, nominal $. Wheat, hard red winter; Rice, Thai
Source: Authors' elaborations on World Bank data, Global Economic Monitor (GEM) Commodities, 2013

Figure 2. Real world food and cereal price indices, 2002–2004=100

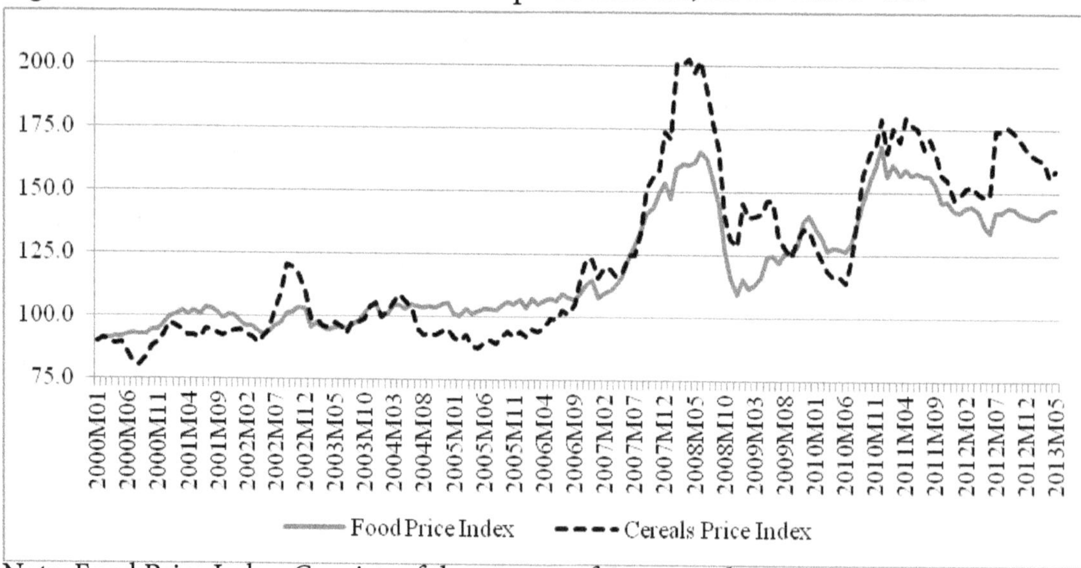

Note: Food Price Index: Consists of the average of 5 commodity group price indices (Cereals, Meat, Dairy, Oils, and Sugar) weighted with the average export shares of each of the groups for 2002–2004: in total, 55 commodity quotations are considered. Cereals Price Index: This index is compiled using the grains and rice price indices weighted by their average trade share for 2002–2004. Source: Authors' elaborations on FAO, 2013.

creasing demand (Haile, Kalkuhl, and von Braun 2013). Surges in food prices are also the consequence of neglected investment in agriculture in many developing countries and the resulting low productivity (World Bank 2007). Furthermore, food prices are expected to increase in the long run, due in part to climate change, which is posing new risks and constraints. Supply and demand forces may cause maize prices to rise by approximately 100 percent by 2050 (Nelson et al. 2010), unless much larger investments in innovation are forthcoming.

At a macro level, loose fiscal policies and expansive monetary policies in many countries have created an environment that favors high commodity prices. Frankel (2008), Svensson (2008), and Algieri (2013) emphasize the high responsiveness of agriculture prices to monetary policy changes and hence to interest-rate maneuvers. There are two channels through which interest rates affect food commodity prices. The first operates through physical demand: low interest rates stimulate inventory demand because they decrease the cost of carrying inventories. This, in turn, raises commodity prices. The second channel operates through investment-fund activity, the so-called financialization of commodities, a highly debated topic that can be considered a new driver of commodity prices. Investment–fund activity, which has been increasing over the course of the last decade, exceeded US$330 billion during 2012, according to Barclay Hedge, which tracks developments in the hedge fund industry (World Bank 2013). Most of the funds have been invested in energy and agricultural commodity markets. Thus, food and financial markets have become more interlinked. These links pose new risks and uncertainties for the poor in developing countries, since these funds have sufficiently large weight to unbalance the market, which could lead to excessive price spikes and to distortions of the price-discovery mechanism (Gilbert and Pfuderer 2012).

Despite the attractiveness of commodities as asset class in times of low interest rates and high risks of inflation, investments into commodity futures are also influenced by speculation or more complex portfolio diversification strategies. Speculation may be approximated by the activity of non-commercial traders who—in contrast to commercial traders who use futures markets for hedging business risks—are supposed to be risk taking. Index funds can be used as an instrument to speculate on price movements, to hedge against price fluctuations, or to diversify a portfolio. Therefore, there is controversy whether their activity can be regarded as speculation (Stoll and Whaley 2010).

The empirical evidence of the impact of financial market on food commodity market is mixed and depends on the econometric methods and proxies used in the analyses (see Table 1 for an overview). In general, all studies report a significant and positive contemporaneous correlation between speculation or index fund activity and price *levels*, and disagree in the magnitude and existence of a causal relationship. As price movements influence expectations, they might also influence speculative activities. Hence, many studies use Granger-causality tests to evaluate if there is a one-way relationship, a two-way relationship, or no specific relationship between price changes and speculative activity. Granger-causality tests do not suggest systematic and strong evidence: either they establish causality only for very few commodities or they confirm causality only for short time periods (some include the years 2006–2008). The commodities and time periods where causality is detected further differ between studies. While Gilbert

Table 1. Empirical analyses of financial market impacts on agricultural commodity prices and volatility

Considered driver	Methodological approach		
	Granger-causality	**Market fundamentals**	**Other**
Impact on price level (or returns)			
Speculation	Robles, Torero, and Braun (2009)	von Braun and Tadesse (2012)	Stoll and Whaley (2010)
	Brunetti, Buyuksahin, and Harris (2011)	Algieri (2013)	
	Stoll and Whaley (2010)		
	Gilbert (2010a,b)		
Index-Funds	Gilbert and Pfuderer (2012)	Gilbert (2010)	Irwin and Sanders (2012)
	Aulerich, Irwin, and Garcia (2010)		Henderson, Pearson, and Wang (2012)
	Gilbert (2009)		Sanders and Irwin (2010)
			Gilbert (2009)
Financialization			Tang and Xiong (2012)
Impact on price volatility			
Speculation	Algieri (2012)	von Braun and Tadesse (2012)	
	Brunetti, Buyuksahin, and Harris (2011)		
Index-Funds	Aulerich, Irwin, and Garcia (2010)		Irwin and Sanders (2012)
Financialization		von Braun and Tadesse (2012)	Tang and Xiong (2012)
			Grosche (2013)

Note: Source: Authors' elaboration. Legend: red—substantial evidence; shaded—weak or mixed evidence, gray—no evidence.

(2010a) gives a strong evidence of Granger-causality—using a novel index fund activity measure—others question whether Granger-causality tests are appropriate as they postulate that financial markets act slowly and do not process all available information quickly (Grosche 2012).

Studies using other identification strategies to investigate causality find a stronger relationship between speculation, index fund activity, and financialization on price levels. Some use information on supply and demand fundamentals to control for expectations (Tadesse et al. 2013), others use instrumental variables (Gilbert 2010a,b) or focus on specific financial products where anticipation of short-term price movements can be ruled out (Henderson, Pearson, and Wang 2012). Despite some evidence for the impact of financial market activities on price levels, the impact of speculation and index-funds on volatility is contested. Speculation of informed traders is considered to improve the price-formation process and increase liquidity in commodity markets which could smoothen transactions. Some studies report even a significant volatility decreasing effect of speculation (Brunetti, Buyuksahin, and Harris 2011) and index funds (Irwin and Sanders 2012). On the other hand, Tang and Xiong (2012) find that agricultural commodities have become more inter-linked to other asset markets, in particular energy markets; Grosche (2013) and Tadesse et al. (2013) suggest that stock markets, real estate, and bond markets as well as financial crises influence the volatility of agricultural commodities; and Algieri (2012) finds a bi-directional causality between price volatility and speculation, in the sense that price volatility can be caused by arbitrage and speculation, and price volatility itself can cause a rise in arbitrage and speculation.

Further macroeconomic factors that led to higher prices are (1) the depreciation of the US dollar, the currency of choice for most international commodity transactions, which put an upward pressure on demand from non-US dollar commodity consumers and producers (Gilbert 2010a,b; Algieri 2013), and (2) restrictive trade policies. A host of authors (Yang et al. 2008; Dawe and Slayton 2010; Headey 2011; Sharma 2011; Martin and Anderson 2012) have shown that the sequence of restrictions and bans implemented by exporting countries such as India, Thailand, China, and Russia have exacerbated price increases. This is because trade restrictions protect domestic consumers from the effects of high prices at the expense of a shrinking global market which hits consumers in other countries. When, in fact, many countries adopt the same strategy, the world market becomes highly volatile (Gouel 2013). Between 2008 and 2011, 29 countries imposed export restrictions on food (Table 2) which was both a cause and a consequence of high price volatility.

Another new driver of food prices is the diversion of some food commodities, in particular maize, to the production of biofuels. Indeed, the rapid expansion of biofuel production in the past decade due to subsidies, mandates, and, in part, due to higher fuel prices has created new linkages and trade-offs. Rising demand for biofuel feedstock has introduced a fundamental change in food-price determination. In the United States, the share of the maize harvest diverted to ethanol production increased from 15 percent in 2006 to 40 percent in 2012 (USDA 2013). Several studies estimate that biofuel policies increased corn prices by more than 30 percent and other grains and food items by 10–20 percent (Hochman et al. 2011).

Table 2. Restrictive export policies (from January 1, 2008 to October 11, 2011)

Export bans	Export taxes and restrictions	Export licenses and quotas
Chad (2010)	China (2008)	Tanzania (2010)
Cote d'Ivoire (2011)	India (2008)	Kazakhstan (2008)
Egypt (2008–2011)	Nepal (2008)	Pakistan (2010)
Ethiopia (2008–2010)	Vietnam (2008)	Vietnam (2008)
Guinea (2011)	Argentina (2008)	Ukraine (2010–2011)
Guinea (2008)	Bolivia (2008)	
Kenya (2011)	Belarus (2008)	
Kenya (2008)	Russia (2008)	
Liberia (2008)	Ukraine (2010–2012)	
Malawi (2008–2009)	Ukraine (2010)	
Tanzania (2008–2011)	Ukraine (2008)	
Zambia (2008–2009)		
Bangladesh (2009–2010)		
Bangladesh (2008)		
Cambodia (2008)		
India (2008–2011)		
Kazakhstan (2011)		
Kazakhstan (2010)		
Kazakhstan (2008)		
Myanmar (2008)		
Nepal (2008)		
Pakistan (2009–2010)		
Syria (2008)		
Argentina (2008)		
Bolivia (2010)		
Bolivia (2008)		
Brazil (2011)		
Ecuador (2008)		
Moldova (2011)		
Russia (2010–2011)		
Russia (2008)		
Serbia (2011)		
Serbia (2008)		

Source: Authors' elaborations on FAO, GIEWS Country Policy Monitoring, July 2013.

Legend: black – eastern European countries; Green – Latin American countries; Blue – African countries; Red – Asian countries.

Figure 3. Main Drivers of Food-Price Volatility

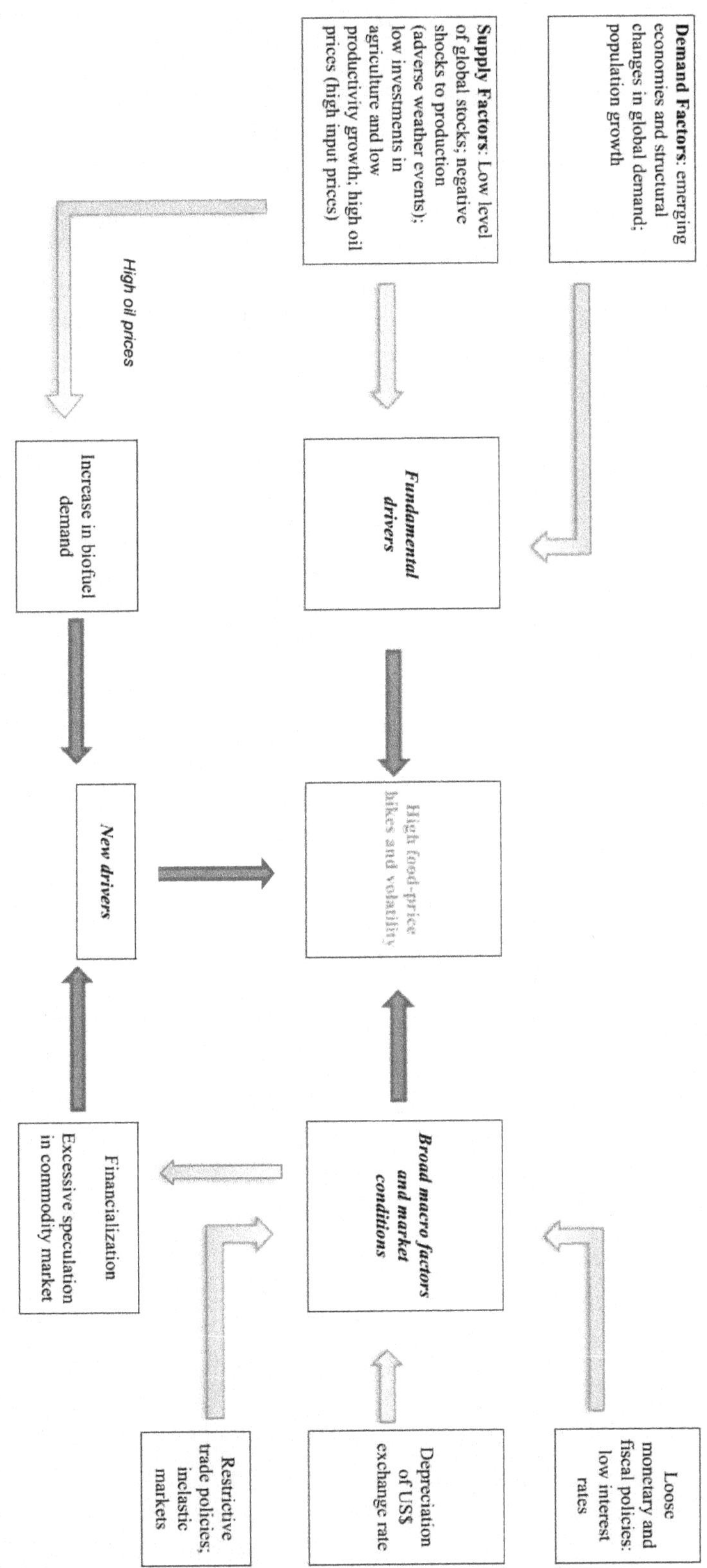

Source: Derived by authors

Main consequences of hikes in commodity prices

The surging prices of agricultural commodities and extreme price volatility at international markets were transmitted to many developing countries. Several analyses reveal that, depending on the country and commodity, 10–40 percent of international price changes are transmitted to the local level (Robles 2011; Greb et al. 2012; Ianchovichina, Loening, and Wood 2012). The transmission to grain prices is typically higher than the transmission to the food price basket released by the official national statistical agencies. As the latter contains many processed foods and non-staples, it is less representative for poor people. Figure 4 shows the maximum transmission from several international commodity prices to domestic food price indices (which are despite their shortcomings the only available price indices with almost global coverage). As grains and unprocessed food have a higher share in the food basket of developing countries, food price indices in developing countries respond stronger to international prices. Although some countries like India could successfully isolate the domestic grain market from the international market through high trade barriers, their food prices are notwithstanding linked to international prices through oilseeds and vegetable oil prices.

The strong transmission of international price shocks undermines food security—that is, the availability of and access to sufficient amounts of healthy food and good nutrition, adversely affects a country's political stability, and generates additional ripple effects, which will be discussed below.

Hunger, malnutrition, and food crises

Price spikes that result in real income changes require poor people to reduce calorie intake or the quality of their diets (e.g., Torlesse, Kiess, and Bloem 2003). Since childhood nutrition is a key element for children's cognitive and physical development and for their productivity and potential earning ability as adults, the health and economic consequences of the lack of food and deprived diets are lifelong for both individuals and society (Black et al. 2008; Victora et al. 2008). Therefore, even when several price shocks end, the adverse effects for the poor can still impair physical and mental capacities, thus resulting in human suffering and economic costs to society.

Data on undernourishment and malnutrition is highly fragmented, and the recent food crisis shed light on this issue. In particular, the numbers reported by the FAO for undernourished people are estimates, which do not account for the decrease in diet quality and related health effects (FAO 2012). Although at the global level, the percentage of people who are undernourished or affected from food insecurity has declined since 2007, the recent price spikes have temporally and locally reversed this tendency or reduced the success in improving nutrition (Tiwari and Zaman 2010; Anríquez, Daidone, and Mane 2013).

Using global panel data, Kalkuhl et al. (2013b) find a significant relationship between the volatility of food prices (measured as the coefficient of variation of food prices) and anthropometric indicators of undernourishment. Their estimated coefficients suggest that each doubling of volatility increases the prevalence of underweight of children under 5 years old by 0.6–1.3 % (depending on model specification) and the prevalence of stunt-

Figure 4. Pass-through elasticities of international food and commodity prices to national food price indices

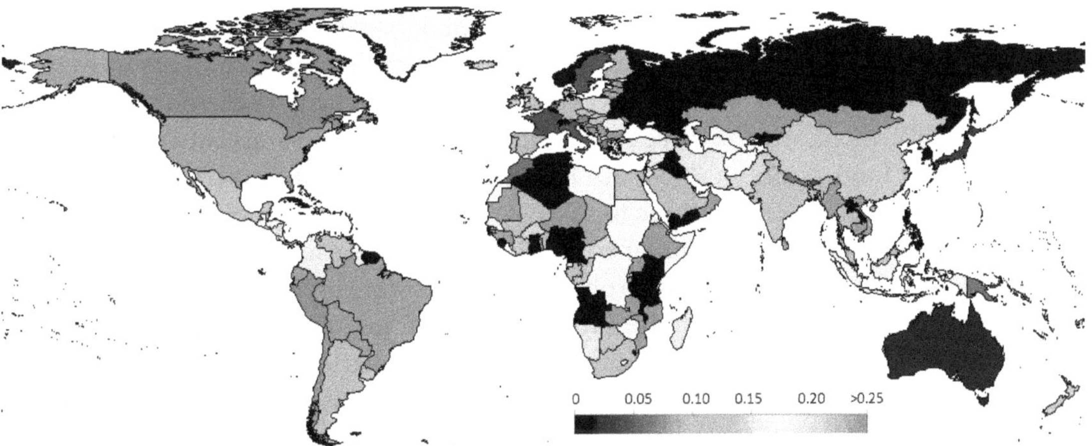

Note: A pass-through elasticity of 0.20 implies that domestic food prices increase in the long run by 20 percent if one of the international reference prices (or price indices) increases by 100 percent. The analysis is based on a large set of international grain and oilseed prices, aggregated price indices as well as futures prices. Domestically, national food price indices are considered. Pass-through elasticities which were not significant at the 5% level were set to zero. Source: Kalkuhl (2013).

ed children by 0.1–0.7 %. Although these elasticities seem to be small, food price volatility in developing countries can more than triple within one year. Furthermore, the estimated elasticities are average effects over a large set of countries, implying that the effects on countries with chronic nutrition problems are likely to be larger.

When rates of hunger and malnutrition rise sharply at local, national, or global levels, a food crisis occurs. "This distinguishes a food crisis from chronic hunger, although food crises are far more likely among populations already suffering from prolonged hunger and malnutrition. A food crisis is usually set off by a shock to either supply or demand for food and often involves a sudden spike in food prices" (Timmer 2010). Therefore, the three recent acute spikes of food prices in 2008, 2011, and 2012 can be understood as three food-price crises in sequence. The simultaneous economic crisis of 2007–2008 has probably affected food security further although empirical analyses on this issue are scant[4].

Threats to political stability

Strong increases in food prices can catalyze unrests, violent conflicts, and political instability. In developing countries with widespread poverty, political organizations may be alleged to have a critical role in food security. Failure to deliver security undermines the actual reason for the existence of the political system. When this situation materializes, the resulting protests can echo several causes, broadening the scope of the protest and masking the immediate trigger for the unrest (Lagi, Bertrand, and Bar-Yam 2011). During the first hikes in food prices registered in 2008, many governments underestimated their impacts on political security. From January 2007 to June 2008, food protests—strikes, demonstrations, and riots over food-related issues—occurred in more than 40 countries, with some countries experiencing multiple occurrences and a high degree of violence (von Braun 2008; Schneider 2008).

While "classical" food riots occurred in the countryside and involved the rural poor, "modern" food riots concentrate in cities, involve the urban middle class, and are more political oriented as they focus on the role of governments in guaranteeing food security (Bellemare 2011). The patterns of relationships between the food-price crisis and political conflicts and food riots in 2008 differ from those in 2011. In 2011 the responses of protesters and governments were more complex and sophisticated than in 2008. While protests in 2011 were again partly triggered by food-price inflation, such as in Egypt, Tunisia, and recently in Brazil, coordinated protests were increasingly facilitated by improved communications through new social media such as Twitter and Facebook (Ciezadlo 2011). These riots can no longer be equated with historical bread riots or even the massive 2008 food protests; rather, they became symptoms of empowerment and part of more systematic uprisings (Bush 2010). Protests quickly turned to much larger events involving regime changes.

Empirical analyses based on cross-country observations over several decades suggest a causal relationship between food price increases and the likelihood of unrest and protests (Arezki and Bruckner 2011; Bellemare 2011) although such events depend also on the surrounding economic and political conditions. For

[4] Brinkman et al. (2010) discuss the impact of the economic crisis on food security and provide some simulations. There is, however, evidence that economic crises can increase food insecurity (e.g. Block et al. 2004)) and child mortality (Baird, Friedman, and Schady 2010)

a large set of countries and a period of six decades, Arezki and Bruckner (2011) find that increasing food prices are associated with contemporaneous changes of political regimes to become more authoritarian and with increased civil conflicts. Whether the long-term effects of food price induced political instability are positive or negative is therefore difficult to assess and requires a differentiated and country-specific analysis.

Ripple effects

Higher grain costs and food crises have large, economic ripple effects: they first put additional pressure on non-core inflation—that is, the inflation of food and energy prices. This occurs because of substitution effects (if prices of one staple increase demand for other staple increases provoking secondary price increases). But grain prices are also linked to meat and processed food through the costs of production. Put differently, several products can increase in price as a consequence of an increase in grain prices. Non-core inflation in turn put pressures on wages and other consumption goods in particular in developing countries or emerging economies (IMF 2011; Durevall, Loening, and Birru 2013; Hui 2013). Central banks, however, typically fight only non-core inflation with monetary policy interventions neglecting food price changes as root cause of price increases (IMF 2011).

Another ripple effect of food crises is the loss of trust in trade and the reemergence of self-sufficiency policies in many countries in an effort to curtail the effects of higher global prices on domestic prices and ease the impacts on particular groups. This includes limits or bans on food exports and increasing import tariffs, as depicted in Table 2. The latter points to three main stylized facts. First, African and Asian countries have adopted the largest number of restricted policies, while Latin America has the lowest number of restrictions. Second, the most-used measures were export bans. Third, all the countries tend to adopt more tariff barriers than non-tariff barriers. The latter may be related to product standards, process standards, certification, registration and testing procedures, packaging, mark-up, labeling, and environmental barriers. Trade restrictions play a direct role in exacerbating food price spikes. Indeed, as major regional producers reduce the regional and global supply of grain, they become responsible for increased price volatility and other negative consequences for import-dependent neighboring countries. These countries will forgo benefits from trade and externalize domestic fluctuations in supplies, further increasing volatilities in international markets (Gouel 2013). Put another way, export restrictions may reduce food-shortage risks in the short term, but they result in trade policy failures, they make the global market smaller and more volatile, and they have adverse impacts on import-dependent partners.

Prices, risk, and production

The excessive commodity price movements during 2007 and 2011 were associated with high price risk for producers: Farmers without access to futures contracts or other price insurance mechanisms face the risk of high losses if increasing prices fall suddenly. The high price volatility in wheat and maize leads to less area cultivated (Chavas and Holt 1990; Liang et al. 2011; Haile, Kalkuhl, and von Braun 2013) and to less investments into yield-increasing inputs (Haile and Kalkuhl

2013). Hence, price incentive effects from price spikes that would lead eventually to higher production are partly hampered by increasing price risks.

The fast-rising food prices have further increased commercial pressure on land and, implicitly, on water resources for agriculture (von Braun 2010, Cotula et al. 2011). It is, therefore, not surprising that prices for farmland have risen throughout the world in recent years. The global expansion of land markets is driven mostly by domestic players, but also partly by the growing transnational acquisition of land by financially strong investors, including some that act directly or indirectly on behalf of countries attempting to improve their food security, in view of domestic scarcity of land and water. In many developing countries, land rights are not well defined, which can lead to conflicts between the local population and investors (German, Schoneveld, and Mwangi 2011).

The Cures

Two kinds of policy actions to respond to high and volatile food prices must be distinguished: those largely in the domain of national governments and those best handled at the international level and requiring attention by global actors. Actions are needed at both levels. The focus in this paper is on global actions. Such actions should include the following:

1.Policies to improve agricultural productivity in the medium and long-run, targeting investments in agriculture, including research and development (R&D) and innovation, measures to improve land and water policies, and coordinated engagement to deal with climate change in order to address the root causes of price volatility;

2. Policies to reduce excessive volatility, embracing open trade, flexible bioenergy policies, grain reserves, and regulation of commodity markets;

3. Social protections and nutrition policies to alleviate chronic and acute undernourishment.

4. A redesign of international institutional arrangements and organizations for food security to address collective action failures

1: Policies to improve agricultural productivity

Spending on agricultural R&D is an important investment for promoting growth and reducing poverty (World Bank 2007). Disseminating new technology in agriculture requires substantial up-front investments in the foundations of effective technology utilization—that is, rural education, infrastructure, and extension services. As developing countries lack funds for research expenditures, a science and technology initiative may be necessary to accelerate innovation and prevent further increases in agricultural prices. If investments in public agricultural research were doubled, agricultural output would increase significantly, and millions of people would emerge from poverty (von Braun et al. 2008). "Best bets" include innovative programs that would revitalize yield growth in intensive rice and wheat systems in Asia, increase small-scale fish production, address threatening pests like virulent wheat rust, breed maize that can be grown in drought-prone areas, and scale up biofortified food crops.

2: Policies to prevent extreme price volatility

A second set of policies should aim at stabilizing food prices and mitigating extreme volatility. To prevent extreme volatility, it is essential to ensure open trade and guarantee transparent and appropriately regulated market institutions. After deregulating commodity markets in the past decades, it is important to increase transparency of futures markets (providing information on actors and transactions) and prevent excessive price-distorting speculation. Excluding food from speculative futures markets, however, could provoke more volatility and impede the price identification process (Santos 2002; Jacks 2007). Nevertheless, food markets should not be excluded from the appropriate regulation of banking and financial systems, as the staple foods and feed markets (grain and oilseeds) are closely connected to speculative activities in financial markets.

In view of the adverse role of biofuel-subsidy policies for food insecurity in times of tight grain supplies, energy policies need to take food-security consequences, which they currently ignore, into account explicitly. Blending mandates provide low flexibility to reduce biofuel production when food prices are high. As subsidies reduce energy prices and therefore increase energy demand, biofuel subsides are in general a costly and inefficient policy to reduce carbon emissions compared to a carbon tax or emissions trading scheme (Cui et al. 2011; Kalkuhl, Edenhofer, and Lessmann 2013a). When food prices are high, subsidies and mandates for biofuel production should be lowered to reduce pressure on food markets. Second-generation biofuel technologies may further increase the land efficiency of biofuel production and therefore lessen the trade-off between energy and food production (IPCC 2011).

Global collective action for trade and grain policies that enhance food security is needed to overcome the collective action failures in grain markets: The larger the world market, the lower the price variations needed to balance demand and supply. Trade policies should thus encourage greater integration into international markets. A key role could be played by more open trade and stock release policies by India and China, countries that sit on large grain stocks. More trade liberalization in general and in particular by these two nations could improve the global food-security situation (Ganesh-Kumar, Roy, and Gulati 2010). Further cooperation can be achieved in building independent regional or international grain reserves (that include other nutritious foods) exclusively for emergency response and humanitarian assistance. Regional policy bodies, such as the Association of Southeast Asian Nations, the South Asian Association for Regional Cooperation, and African regional and sub-regional bodies have partly implemented joint-reserve policies, which could constitute one step in the proposed direction. A regional set of arrangements, however, is suboptimal and may run into problems of trust in regions with one or two dominating regional powers.

3: Social protection and nutrition policies

Actions related to agricultural production, trade, and reserves are necessary but not sufficient for overcoming the food and nutrition security crisis, which is not just an acute problem, but exacerbates a global chronic problem. As agricultural markets will always exhibit volatile prices due to random production shocks, health and nutrition risks have to be addressed through social transfers and health services. Most of these actions are carried out by national governments, but international support for these investments is also needed, especially in the least-developed countries (Morris, Cogill, and Uauy 2008). Setting priorities in this area requires a sound metric for targeting actions and measuring progress. Policy actions in three priority areas are called for: (1) expand social protection and child nutrition action to protect the basic nutrition of the most vulnerable; (2) take protective actions to mitigate short-term risks (such actions would include cash transfers, pension systems, and employment programs); and (3) adopt preventive health and nutrition interventions to avoid long-term negative consequences.

4: New international institutional arrangements needed

International extreme food price volatility calls for global governance action that requires institutional arrangements, which are currently lacking. If we were to design a global governance system for agriculture, food, and nutrition today, it certainly would not look like the current one. Action is overdue to shape a well-functioning future, global institutional architecture of agriculture and food that is capable to deliver the international public goods for food security, and it actually should limit its tasks to just that, international public goods, and not what national policies are better at delivering. Two institutional re-design mechanisms are needed: (1) a platform that facilitates public goods policy actions and (2) a global assessment mechanism to provide evidence base for strategic directions for action.

Platform for decisions: A legitimate, nimble, and innovative set of strategic bodies to help co-ordinate the actions of others (i.e., some of the existing international organizations) is needed: a *platform* that can facilitate global action as well as government-to-government networks, with inclusion of private sector industry and civil society actors. It should have legalized political authority to watch over and broadly facilitate public goods delivery in support of global agricultural development and food and nutrition security. A candidate could be a truly independently-governed Committee on World Food Security (CFS). It currently lacks independent governance structures and budgetary authorities. A system is only as strong as its weakest parts, so this global strategic body needs to be able to rely on more effective global agencies. For that, the FAO should be re-invented and strengthened to deliver the public goods that facilitate sustainable agricultural intensification and growth under climate change, food security information, and global food safety services. Second, global nutrition policy needs an organizational home and not split among currently five agencies; Third, ***WFP*** needs to be supported to better mitigate and respond to emergency food crises by getting a reliable global food store and funding that permits flexible response. Institutional redesign would be best arranged around focus areas that facilitate IPG delivery in order to facilitate public goods inter-linkages. Three such *focal clusters* of organizational setups may be considered at the level of such a platform: one on food and nutrition security of the poor; a second on protection of natural resources; and a third on enhanced sustainable intensification and productivity growth.

International assessment mechanism: The current and future challenges of agricultural development and food and nutrition security require a strong mechanism for science and research based assessment as a permanent institutional arrangement. A global body tasked with this could be mapped along the lines of the Intergovernmental Panel on Climate Change (IPCC), but avoiding its well known pitfalls from the outset. It needs to have a perspective for the coming two to three decades as the agriculture and food issues are filled with uncertainties and opportunities. It is not a one-off assessment task or a set of studies, but an integral part of a sound international public goods delivery system for agriculture, food- and nutrition security. An independent IPCC-type global research body that communicates academic consensus and scientific uncertainties on agriculture, food, and nutrition is needed for delivering evidence based analyses for action with foresight. This function goes beyond the existing Consultative Group on International Agricultural Research (CGIAR), and calls on the whole international science system related to agriculture, food, and nutrition.

The re-design of the system should be done step by step. The steps could be guided by the above-mentioned cost effectiveness assessments, with adherence to the principles of legitimacy with accountability, effectiveness, and inventiveness. Coming to a meaningful implementation of this re-design option will require leadership. Leadership for change could come from the developing countries via the UN and the G20 which could play a key role to initiate the change.

Conclusions

Food-price volatility deserves much more attention in the policy arena in order to improve food security globally. Governments can act to shield their citizens from higher prices and volatility in world markets by initiating measures to stabilize food prices and by establishing social protection systems that mitigate the impact of high food prices on vulnerable groups. However, since extreme price volatility is an international concern, it does require international action. National actions such as excessively increasing grain stocks or restricting trade are inefficient and make global matters worse. Instead, three groups of policies at the international level should be accomplished: they include coordinated measures to foster production, technology, and private investment in order to allay the root causes of price upsurges; harmonized trade, bioenergy, grain reserves, and financial policies so as to prevent excessive price volatility and speculation in food markets; and targeted social protection and nutrition policies to alleviate undernourishment. The global food governance architecture needs to be redesigned to deliver the public goods components for international food security.

References

Abbott, P.C., C. Hurt, and W.E. Tyner. 2008. *What's Driving Food Prices?* Oak Brook: Farm Foundation. http://www.farmfoundation.org/news/articlefiles/404-ExecSum8.5x11.pdf

Abbott, P.C., C. Hurt, and W.E. Tyner. 2011. *What's Deriving Food Prices in 2011*? Oak Brook: Farm Foundation. https://www.farmfoundation.org/news/articlefiles/105-FoodPrices_web.pdf

Aksoy, A., and A. Isik-Dikmelik. 2008. "Are Low Food Prices Pro-Poor? Net Food Buyers and Sellers in Low-Income Countries." World Bank Policy Research Working Paper Series 4642, June 1, Washington, DC: The World Bank.

Algieri, B. 2012. "Price Volatility, Speculation and Excessive Speculation in Commodity Markets: Sheep or Shepherd Behaviour?" ZEF-Discussion Papers on Development Policy No.166. Center for Development Research, University of Bonn. http://ageconsearch.umn.edu/bitstream/124390/2/DP166.pdf

Algieri, B. 2013. "A Roller Coaster Ride: an Empirical Investigation of the Main Drivers of Wheat Price," ZEF-Discussion Papers on Development Policy No.176, Center for Development Research, University of Bonn. http://www.zef.de/fileadmin/webfiles/downloads/zef_dp/zef_dp_176.pdf

Anríquez, G., S. Daidone, and E. Mane. 2013. "Rising Food Prices and Undernourishment: A Cross-country Inquiry." *Food Policy* 38: 190-202.

Arezki, R., and M. Bruckner. 2011. "Food Prices and Political Instability." IMF Working Paper: WP/11/62. International Monetary Fund. http://www.imf.org/external/pubs/ft/wp/2011/wp1162.pdf

Aulerich, N.M., S.H. Irwin, and P. Garcia. 2010. *The Price Impact of Index Funds in Commodity Futures Markets: Evidence from the CFTC's Daily Large Trader Reporting System*. http://are.berkeley.edu/documents/seminar/Irwin.pdf

Baird, S., J. Friedman, and N. Schady. 2010. "Aggregate Income Shocks and Infant Mortality in the Developing World." *Review of Economics and Statistics* 93: 847-56.

Barrett, C.B. 2008. "Smallholder Market Participation: Concepts and Evidence from Eastern and Southern Africa." *Food Policy* 33: 299-317.

Bellemare, M.F. 2011. "Rising Food Prices, Food Price Volatility, and Political Unrest." MPRA Paper No. 31888. http://mpra.ub.uni-muenchen.de/31888/.

Benson T., N. Minot, J. Pender, M. Robles, and J. von Braun. 2013. "Information to Guide Policy Responses to Higher Global Food Prices: The Data and Analyses Required." *Food Policy* 38: 47–58.

Black, R.E., L.H. Allen, Z.A. Bhutta, L.E. Caulfield, M. de Onis, M. Ezzati, C. Mathers, and J. Rivera. 2008. "Maternal and Child Undernutrition: Global and Regional Exposures and Health Consequences." *The Lancet* 371: 243-60.

Block, S.A., L. Kiess, P. Webb, S. Kosen, R. Moench-Pfanner, M.W. Bloem, and C.P. Timmer. 2004. "Macro Shocks and Micro Outcomes: Child Nutrition during Indonesia's Crisis." *Economics and Human Biology* 2 (1): 21-44.

Brinkman, H.J., S. de Pee, I. Sanogo, L. Subran, and M.W. Bloem. 2010. "High Food Prices and the Global Financial Crisis have Reduced Access to Nutritious Food and Worsened Nutritional Status and Health." *The Journal of Nutrition* 140: 153S-161S.

Brunetti, C., B. Buyuksahin, and J. Harris. 2011. "Speculators, Prices and Market Volatility." Available at SSRN 1736737. http://www.bancaditalia.it/studiricerche/seminari/2011/brunetti/paper-brunetti.pdf

Bush, R. 2010. "Food Riots: Poverty, Power and Protest." *Journal of Agrarian Change* 10: 119-29.

Chavas, J.P., and M.T. Holt. 1990. "Acreage Decisions Under Risk: The Case of Corn and Soybeans." *American Journal of Agricultural Economics* 72: 529-38.

Ciezadlo, A. 2011. "Let them Eat Bread: How Food Subsidies Prevent (and Provoke) Revolutions in the Middle East." *Foreign Affairs* March 23. http://www.foreignaffairs.com/articles/67672/annia-ciezadlo/let-them-eat-bread

Cotula, L., S. Vermeulen, P. Mathieu, and C. Toulmin. 2011. "Agricultural Investment and International Land Deals: Evidence from a Multi-Country Study in Africa." *Food Security* 3: 99-113.

Cui, J., H. Lapan, G. Moschini, and J. Cooper. 2011. "Welfare Impacts of Alternative Biofuel and Energy Policies." *American Journal of Agricultural Economics* 93: 1235-56.

Dawe, D., and T. Slayton. 2010. "The World Rice Market Crisis of 2007–2008." In *The Rice Crisis: Markets, Policies and Food Security*, edited by David Dawe, 15-28. London: FAO of the UN and Earthscan.

Durevall, D., J.L. Loening, and Y.A. Birru. 2013. "Inflation Dynamics and Food Prices in Ethiopia." *Journal of Development Economics* 104: 89-106.

FAO, ***WFP***, and IFAD. 2012. *The State of Food Insecurity in the World 2012. Economic Growth is Necessary but not Sufficient to Accelerate Reduction of Hunger and Malnutrition.* Rome: FAO.

Ferderer, P.J. 1997. "Oil Price Volatility and the Macroeconomy." *Journal of Macroeconomics* 18: 1-26.

Frankel, J.A. 2008. "The Effect of Monetary Policy on Real Commodity Prices." In NBER Chapters.National Bureau of Economic Research, Inc, 291-333.

Ganesh-Kumar, A., D. Roy, and A. Gulati. 2010. "Liberalizing Foodgrains Markets: Experiences, Impact, and Lessons from South Asia." IFPRI Issue Brief 64. Washington, DC: International Food Policy Research Institute. http://www.ifpri.org/sites/default/files/publications/ib64.pdf.

German, L., G. Schoneveld, and E. Mwangi. 2011. "Processes of Large-Scale Land Acquisition by Investors: Case Studies from Sub-Saharan Africa." International Conference on Global Land Grabbing, University of Sussex, 6-8.

Gilbert, C.L. 2010a. "Speculative Influences on Commodity Futures Prices 2006–2008." Discussion Paper 197. United Nations Conference on Trade and Development.

Gilbert, C.L. 2010b. "How to Understand High Food Prices." *Journal of Agricultural Economics* 61: 398-425.

Gilbert, C.L., and S. Pfuderer. 2012. *Index Funds Do Impact Agricultural Prices.* Money, Macro and Finance Study Group Workshop on Commodity Markets, London, Bank of England.

Gilbert, C.L., and S. Pfuderer. Forthcoming. "The Financialization of Food Commodity Markets." *In Handbook on Food: Demand, Supply, Sustainability and Security*, edited by R. Jha, T. Gaiha, and A. Deolalikar.

Gouel, C., 2013. "Food Price Volatility and Domestic Stabilization Policies in Developing Countries." NBER Working Paper

18934. Cambridge, MA: National Bureau of Economic Research.

Greb, F., N. Jamora, C. Mengel, S. von Cramon-Taubadel, S., and N. Würriehausen. 2012. "Price Transmission from International to Domestic Markets." Global Food Discussion Paper 15. Gottingen: GlobalFood.

Grosche, S. 2012. "Limitations of Granger Causality Analysis to Assess the Price Effects from the Financialization of Agricultural Commodity Markets under Bounded Rationality." Institute for Food and Resource Economics Discussion Paper 1. University of Bonn.

Grosche, S. 2013. *Volatility Spillovers between Agricultural Commodity and Financial Asset Markets*. ZEF Volatility Workshop. University of Bonn, February 1.

Haile, M.G., and M. Kalkuhl. 2013. "Agricultural Supply Response to International Food Prices and Price Volatility: A Cross-country Panel Analysis." Annual Meeting, Agricultural and Applied Economics Association, Washington, DC, August 4–6.

Haile, M. G., Kalkuhl, M. and von Braun, J. 2013. "Short-Term Global Crop Acreage Response to International Food Prices and Implications of Volatility." ZEF- Discussion Papers on Development Policy No. 175, February 1. http://ssrn.com/abstract=2226943 or http://dx.doi.org/10.2139/ssrn.2226943

Headey, D. 2011. "Rethinking the Global Food Crisis: The Role of Trade Shocks." *Food Policy* 36: 136-46.

Henderson, B., N. Pearson, and L. Wang. 2012. "New Evidence on the Financialization of Commodity Markets." SSRN 1990828.

HLPE. 2011. "Price Volatility and Food Security." A report by the High Level Panel of Experts on Food Security and Nutrition of the Committee on World Food Security, Rome. http://papers.ssrn.com/sol3/papers.cfm?abstract_id=2226943

Hochman, G., D. Rajagopal, G.R. Timilsina, and D. Zilberman. 2011. "The Role of Inventory Adjustments in Quantifying Factors Causing Food Price Inflation." Policy Research Working Paper 5744. Washington, DC: The World Bank.

Hui, L. 2013. "Research on Impacts Given by Grain Price Fluctuation on Customers in Inflation Period." *Research Journal of Applied Sciences, Engineering and Technology* 5: 4118-22.

Ianchovichina, E., J. Loening, and C. Wood. 2012. "How Vulnerable are Arab Countries to Global Food Price Shocks?" Policy Research Working Paper 6018. Washington, DC: The World Bank. http://ssrn.com/abstract=2031389

Intergovernmental Panel on Climate Change (IPCC). 2011. *Renewable Energy Sources and Climate Change Mitigation: Special Report of the Intergovernmental Panel on Climate Change*. Cambridge University Press.

International Monetary Fund (IMF). 2011. Slowing Growth, Rising Risks. World Economic Outlook (WEO) September. IMF.

Irwin, S.H., and D.R. Sanders. 2012. "Testing the Masters Hypothesis in Commodity Futures Markets." *Energy Economics* 34: 256-69.

Ivanic, M., and W. Martin. 2008. "Implications of Higher Global Food Prices for Poverty in Low-Income Countries." *Agricultural Economics* 39: 405-16.

Jacks, D.S. 2007. "Populists Versus Theorists: Futures Markets and the Volatility of Prices." *Explorations in Economic History* 44: 342-62.

Jacks, D.S., K.H. O'Rourke, and J.G. Williamson. 2011. "Commodity Price Volatility and World Market Integration Since 1700." *Review of Economics and Statistics* 93: 800-13.

James, W.E. 2008. "Food Prices and Inflation in Developing Asia: Is Poverty Reduction Coming to an End?" Special Report. Asian Development Bank.

Kalkuhl, M. 2013. "How Strong Do Global Commodity Prices Influence Domestic Food Prices? A Global Price Transmission Analysis." Center for Development Research.

Kalkuhl, M., O. Edenhofer, and K. Lessmann. 2013a. "Renewable Energy Subsidies: Second-Best Policy or Fatal Aberration for Mitigation?" *Resource and Energy Economics* 35: 217-34.

Kalkuhl, M., L. Kornher, M. Kozicka, P. Boulanger, and M. Torero. 2013b. "Concep- tual Framework on Price Volatility and its Impact on Food and Nutrition Security in the Short Term." FOODSECURE Working Paper No.15.

Lagi, M., K. Bertrand, and Y. Bar-Yam. 2011. "The Food Crises and Political Instability in North Africa and the Middle East." Available at SSRN 1910031.

Liang, Y., J. Corey Miller, A. Harri, and K.H. Coble. 2011. "Crop Supply Response under Risk: Impacts of Emerging Issues on Southeastern US Agriculture." *Journal of Agricultural and Applied Economics* 43 (2): 181-94.

Martin, W., and K. Anderson. 2012. "Export Restrictions and Price Insulation During Commodity Price Booms." *American Journal of Agricultural Economics* 94: 422-27.

Morris, S.S., B. Cogill, and R. Uauy. 2008. "Effective International Action Against Undernutrition: Why has it Proven so Difficult and What can be done to Accelerate Progress?" *The Lancet* 371: 608-21.

Nelson, G.C., M.W. Rosegrant, A. Palazzo, I. Gray, C. Ingersoll, R. Robertson, S. Tokgoz, T. Zhu, T.B. Sulser, C. Ringler, S. Msangi, and L. You. 2010. *Food Security, Farming and Climate Change to 2050: Scenarios, Results, Policy Options*. Washington, DC: International Food Policy Research Institute.

Robles, M. 2011. *Price Transmission from International Agricultural Commodity Markets to Domestic Food Prices: Case Studies in Asia and Latin America*. Washington, DC: IFPRI.

Robles, M., M. Torero, and J. von Braun. 2009. *When Speculation Matters*. IFPRI Issue Breif 57. Washington, DC: International Food Policy Research Institute.

Sanders, D.R., and S.H. Irwin. 2010. "A speculative bubble in commodity futures prices? Cross sectional evidence." *Agricultural Economics* 41: 25-32.

Santos, J. 2002. "Did Futures Markets Stabilise US Grain Prices?" *Journal of Agricultural Economics* 53: 25-36.

Schneider, M. 2008. *"We are Hungry!" A Summary Report of Food Riots, Government Responses, and States of Democracy in 2008.* Development Sociology, Cornell University. http://www.corpethics.org/downloads/Hungry_rpt2008.pdf

Sharma, R. 2011. *Food Export Restrictions: Review of the 2007–2010 Experience and Considerations for Disciplining Restrictive Measures.* Rome: FAO.

Stoll, H., and R. Whaley. 2010. *Commodity Index Investing: Speculation or Diversification?* SSRN 1633908.

Svensson, L. 2008. *The Effect of Monetary Policy on Real Commodity Prices: Comment By John Y. Campbell.* NBER, University of Chicago.

Tadesse, G., B. Algieri, M. Kalkuhl, J. von Braun. 2013. "Drivers and Triggers of International Food Price Spikes and Volatility." *Food Policy, first-online.*

Tang, K., and W. Xiong. 2012. "Index Investment and the Financialization of Commodities." *Financial Analysts Journal* 68: 54-74.

Timmer, C.P. 2010. "Preventing Food Crises Using a Food Policy Approach." *The Journal of Nutrition* 140: 224S-228S.

Tiwari, S., and H. Zaman. 2010. "The Impact of Economic Shocks on Global Undernourishment." Policy Research Working Paper 5215. Poverty Reduction and Economic Management Network. Poverty Reduction and Equity Unit. Washington, DC: The World Bank.

Torlesse, H., L. Kiess, and M.W. Bloem. 2003. "Association of Household Rice Expenditure with Child Nutritional Status Indicates a Role for Macroeconomic Food Policy in Combating Malnutrition." *The Journal of Nutrition* 133: 1320-25.

Trostle, R. 2008. "Global Agricultural Supply and Demand: Factors Contributing to the Recent Increase in Food Commodity Prices." *Outlook* (WRS-0801). Economic Research Service. United States Department of Agriculture (USDA).

United States Department of Agriculture (USDA). 2013. Feedgrains Database. http://www.ers.usda.gov/data-products/feed-grains-database.aspx#.Ug3tUhaBKX0

Victora, C.G., L. Adair, C. Fall, P.C. Hallal, R. Martorell, L. Richter, H.S. Sachdev, H.S., and for the Maternal and Child Undernutrition Study Group. 2008. "Maternal and Child Undernutrition: Consequences for Adult Health and Human Capital." *The Lancet* 371 (9609): 340-57.

von Braun, J. 2008. *Food and Financial Crises: Implications for Agriculture and the Poor.* Free downloads from International Food Policy Research Institute (IFPRI). http://www.ifpri.org/sites/default/files/pubs/pubs/agm08/jvb/jvbagm2008.pdf

von Braun, J. 2010. ""Land Grabbing" Ursachen und Konsequenzen internationaler Landakquirierung in Entwicklungsländern." *Zeitschrift für Außen- und Sicherheitspolitik* 3 (3): 299-307. http://www.springerlink.com/content/q86j765nrw8l0335/fulltext.pdf

von Braun, J., S. Fan, R. Meinzen-Dick, M.W. Rosegrant, and A.N. Pratt. 2008. *International Agricultural Research for*

Food Security, Poverty Reduction, and the Environment: What to Expect from Scaling up CGIAR Investments and"Best Bet" Programs. Consultative Group on International Agricultural Research (CGIAR).

World Bank. 2007. *World Development Report 2008: Agriculture for Development.* Washington, DC: The World Bank.

World Bank. 2013. *Global Economic Prospects, Commodity Market Annex.* Washington, DC: The World Bank.

Yang, J., H. Qiu, J. Huang, and S. Rozelle. 2008. "Fighting Global Food Price Rises in the Developing World: the Response of China and its Effect on Domestic and World Markets." *Agricultural Economics* 39: 453-64.

Coping With Climate Change: a Food Policy Approach[1]

C. Peter Timmer[2]

The early drafts of Food Policy Analysis were stimulated by the attention to high food prices following the world food crisis in 1973–74, and the fears of a repeat in 1979–80. But by the fourth full draft, in 1982, it became apparent that surpluses were returning to world food markets. A volume predicated on a world running out of food would have been out of date before the ink was dry, and a full-scale revamping of the analytical messages was needed. After a nearly complete re-write, the new theme, which has stood the test of 30 years of market fluctuations, was the need for flexibility to cope with market instability. That message is even more relevant now, as we learn to cope with a new source of instability—climate change. Such flexibility is not a natural feature of domestic policymaking, in the food sector or elsewhere, and providing the analytical tools for understanding how to create flexible responses turned out to be a real challenge. The task in this paper is to ask specifically how climate change would alter the basic message of Food Policy Analysis. Virtually all of the analysis was focused on national policies and domestic markets, an approach that seems problematical for preventing or mitigating climate change, but entirely appropriate for designing adaptation strategies. Climate change is imposing itself as a reality via the increased probability of extreme weather events in general, and also on both global and localized food security outcomes in particular. The ecosystem services provided by the climate are essential for all agricultural production. The most important effects of climate change on agriculture are likely to include a net global loss of agricultural land, changing crop suitability, an increase in the frequency of natural disasters, and greater temporal and geographic variance in production. It will also have negative effects on other areas of agriculture broadly interpreted—reducing the carrying capacity of many rangelands and posing threats to fisheries and aquaculture production systems. Climate change is expected to have highly variable effects on different regions; tropical and equatorial regions will bear the heaviest burdens, with some gains in yields and land availability in temperate regions. Since rural poverty is concentrated in tropical and, in South Asia, coastal areas, climate change is expected to have a disproportionate effect on the already vulnerable. The challenge is to design, analyze, and implement in-country "climate-smart agriculture" adaptation projects and programs, which are now part of the food policy agenda, as well as to improve the openness to trade in agricultural commodities to even out geographical instability. Designing appropriate policies for bio-fuels also needs to be on the analytical agenda.

Keywords: climate change, food policy analysis, food price, biofuel and agriculture

[1] This paper was prepared for the Australian Agricultural and Resource Economics Society (AARES) meetings in Sydney, February 2013. Some of the observations on *Food Policy Analysis* appeared in Timmer (2010b). I would like to thank Marshall Burke, Wally Falcon, Casey Friedman, Joanne Gaskell, David Lobell, and Roz Naylor for very helpful comments and suggestions. These colleagues all know far more than I do about climate change, and I am learning a lot from them. However, I remain responsible for the views and shortcomings in this essay.

[2] Thomas D. Cabot Professor of Development Studies, emeritus, Harvard University; Non-resident fellow, Center for Global Development, Washington, DC.

Introduction

It has been 30 years since *Food Policy Analysis* (Timmer, Falcon, and Pearson 1983) was published and more than 35 years since the initial outline for the book was circulated among the authors. It is fair to say that the volume has been very influential in thinking about food policy issues since its publication, and it remains in use as a textbook for a number of university courses. Its academic success is a bit surprising because the audience was not primarily university faculty (for whom it seemed too simplistic in methodology and too anecdotal in presentation). Instead, we targeted the message at practitioners, an ill-defined group of analysts in need of an understanding of how a complicated and interconnected food system actually worked. Training these practitioners has turned out to be the main mission of the book, and one that has continuing resonance.

The early drafts of *Food Policy Analysis* (henceforth FPA) were stimulated by the attention to high food prices following the world food crisis in 1973–74, and the fears of a repeat in 1979–80. But by the fourth full draft, in 1982, it became apparent that surpluses were returning to world food markets. A volume predicated on a world running out of food would have been out of date before the ink was dry, and a full-scale revamping of the analytical messages was needed. After a substantial rewrite, the new theme, which has stood the test of 30 years of market fluctuations, was the need for flexibility to cope with market instability. That message is even more relevant now, as we learn to cope with a new source of instability—climate change.

Such flexibility is not a natural feature of domestic policymaking, in the food sector or elsewhere, and providing the analytical tools for understanding how to create flexible responses both to high and low price environments turned out to be a real challenge. But the relevance of the approach remains to this day, accounting for the continued usefulness of an analytical guidebook that is three decades old.

The Basic Message

There was no mistaking the ambitiousness of the primary goal of FPA: rapid and sustained poverty reduction. At the time of drafting, there was not even agreement in the development profession that such a goal was feasible. Paul Streeten had published First Things First: Meeting Basic Human Needs in 1982, eloquently arguing that rapid growth was not possible and that development strategy needed to focus on providing basic needs to the poor. The focus of FPA on more rapid economic growth and the policies to enhance efficiency that would bring it about were controversial for a volume that took poverty seriously.

But FPA argued that growth was not enough. There were four basic food policy objectives, and all four were important:

1. Faster economic growth (the "efficiency" objective).

2. More equal distribution of income from that growth (the "welfare" objective).

3. A guaranteed nutritional floor for the poor (the "safety net" objective).

4. Secure availability and stable prices in food markets (the "food security" objective).

[3] Although long out of print, the volume remains available on-line at a Stanford University website: http://www.stanford.edu/group/FRI/indonesia/documents/foodpolicy/fronttoc.fm.html.

Clearly, there can be trade-offs (and overlap) among these objectives, and substantial analysis of a country's food system was necessary to understand, if even roughly, the magnitudes of the trade-offs. The central organizing theme of the analysis was the "food price dilemma," an explicit recognition that a single market-clearing food price could not satisfy all four objectives simultaneously—a "pure" market solution would not work. Additional policy instruments were needed, but they all needed to operate compatibly with market prices. If readers came away with only one lesson from reading FPA, it was the centrality of food prices—and the signals they sent to farmers, traders, consumers, and finance ministers. The behavior of these decision-making agents dictated market outcomes, but also responded to those market outcomes. The "macro" food system that food policy analysts needed to understand encompassed microbehavior on the farm and in the household, market-level behavior by traders, processors, and retailers, and macroeconomic responses by policymakers. The essential message from FPA was that such understanding, in most circumstances, could not come from complicated models that tried to capture econometrically all the behavioral and market relationships. Instead, the understanding needed to come from a simpler "vision" of how the food system operated. This vision was partly created by the framework and analytical discussion in FPA itself, but more importantly, from the data and simple analysis that practitioners were urged to generate.

With more than three decades of hindsight, it is easy to see several themes that received little attention in FPA but which would require extensive treatment today. Gender played a minor role in the analysis, reflecting the dominance of the "unitary household" model of farm and household decision making at the time (a model that still has considerable relevance, especially in East and Southeast Asia). Further treatment of intra-household decision making, especially with respect to nutrient intake and schooling decisions, is now possible. A "behavioral" perspective would add power to efforts to understand formation of expectations, attitudes toward risk, as well as participation of farmers and households in financial markets. With this behavioral understanding should also come a much more useful political economy framework for understanding policy choices, a topic explicitly left out of FPA (Timmer 2012). Neither "environment" nor "sustainable" appears in the index (although "petroleum prices" have three entries), much less the problems looming from climate change. All should be incorporated into the analysis now. The task in this paper is to ask specifically how climate change would alter the basic message of FPA.

Virtually all of the analysis was focused on national policies and domestic markets, an approach that seems problematical for preventing or mitigating climate change, but entirely appropriate for designing adaptation strategies (Lobell and Burke 2010). The international linkages to these markets were stressed and analyzed, but nearly all food policy interventions are designed and implemented by domestic actors. There are no international "food policymakers," unless you count individuals such as Bill Gates or Jim Kim, who have money and speeches to give, but not policy levers to pull. The food crisis of 2008 saw a renewal of this domestic policy focus, despite the arguably larger role now played by

4 In the late 1970s and early 1980s there was serious debate over whether the earth was warming or cooling.

global integration of factor and commodity markets. And the prospects for global action on climate change now seem dim[5].

The changing global environment

The international context for domestic food policy decision making has changed substantially since FPA was drafted in the early 1980s. Six basic trends stand out:

1. The last four decades have seen surprisingly rapid economic growth, especially in Asia, with hundreds of millions of people pulled out of poverty. The strong connection between inclusive economic growth, especially in rural areas, and rapid reduction of poverty was simply not apparent in the empirical record in the early 1980s. The East Asian Miracle (World Bank 1993) did not appear for another decade. This rapid growth validated the central theme of FPA, which was the unsustainability of poverty reduction efforts without higher economic productivity of unskilled, especially rural, labor. That theme remains powerfully relevant today.

2. A communications revolution at both the household and international levels has radically reduced transactions costs and increased access to knowledge. Again, the centrality in FPA of markets and price formation to understanding food policy design and implementation received a boost as marketing margins narrowed under improved and more informed competition.

[5] As all of my Stanford colleagues pointed out, some countries are large enough that domestic policies have global impact: deforestation in Brazil and Indonesia, use of coal in China, the "Asian Brown Cloud" over India, and use of corn for bio-fuel production in the United States are obvious examples. The absence of "global food policymakers" does not rule out the role of international institutions such as WTO or FAO in influencing global food security.

Consumers and farmers both benefited 1. Consumers and farmers both benefited from more competitive local food markets. The "supermarket revolution" has merely accelerated these changes (Timmer 2009b, Reardon and Timmer 2012).

3. Global financial markets became interested in "emerging economies." The early 1980s were an era of fixed exchange rates, tight controls on the flow of foreign capital, and virtually no financial intermediation beyond state banks. At first, the influx of foreign capital in the 1990s was welcomed as a sign of confidence, but except for foreign direct investment in "real" assets such as factories and real estate, the global financial interest in emerging economies was a two-edged sword. A rapid influx could cause currency appreciation and a loss of competitiveness; its rapid exit when the economy started to decline or foreign investors saw better opportunities elsewhere caused a crisis in local financial markets. Global financial integration came with very poorly understood risks, and 2009 demonstrated them clearly. The growth of foreign investments in land to produce food and/or bio-fuels for export—so-called land-grabs—is controversial, but at least the capital cannot leave the country quickly. The injection of new capital into agriculture in poor countries may not be all bad.

4. The rapid emergence in the 1990s of China and India as global growth engines meant a gradual shift in the drivers of demand for commodities and natural resources. Advanced economies had become more knowledge-driven and less dependent on energy, metals, and other basic commodities—including food commodities—to fuel their economic growth. The price depression for nearly all commodities in the 1980s and 1990s reinforced the view that

the future depended on value added from skills and knowledge, not from exploitation of natural resources. But industrialization, especially as practiced by China and India, is a very intensive user of natural resources (and producer of greenhouse gases). By the turn of the millennium it was increasingly clear that the growth path of developing countries was the primary driver of commodity prices, starting with energy prices but quickly extending to food prices. The Malthusian challenge was back, but with two decades of neglected investments in raising agricultural productivity, the challenge is turning out to be hard to meet.

5. High energy prices have turned out to be a "game changer" for agriculture and the food economy. Once oil prices were high enough to justify using sugar, maize, or vegetable oils to produce gasoline or diesel substitutes, agricultural commodity prices became directly linked to oil prices. The concern to reduce emissions of greenhouse gases to mitigate climate change provided ample motivation to U.S. and European legislatures to mandate the use of domestic food crops to produce liquid fuels. The combination of legislative mandates, which provided essential risk coverage to investors in bio-fuel facilities, and high oil prices, which provided market-based incentives, led to a new set of linkages between agriculture and the energy sector[6]. There had long been a link on the supply side, as energy prices affected fertilizer costs, fuel costs for tractors and trucks, and the economics of global supply chains. The new link was through the demand side. Higher prices for energy translated directly into greater demand for food commodities to convert into liquid fuels.

6. Climate change is imposing itself as a reality on the increased probability of extreme weather events in general, but also on both global and localized food security outcomes in particular. The ecosystem services provided by the climate are a sine qua non for all agricultural production—photosynthesis remains the most efficient way to capture solar energy for human use. The most important effects of climate change on agriculture are likely to include a net global loss of agricultural land, changing crop suitability, and an increase in the frequency of natural disasters. It will also have negative effects on other areas of agriculture broadly interpreted; climate change will reduce the carrying capacity of many rangelands and pose threats to fisheries and aquaculture production systems.

Climate change is expected to have highly variable effects on different regions; tropical and equatorial regions will bear the heaviest burdens, with Sub-Saharan Africa probably facing the greatest challenges, with some gains in yields and land availability in temperate regions[7]. Since rural poverty is concentrated in tropical and, in South Asia, coastal areas, climate change is expected to have a disproportionate effect on the already vulnerable. The growing urbanization of poverty, the result of dysfunctional structural transformations (especially in Africa and India), may change the geographic incidence of the impact of climate change on the poor, but probably not the overall level (Ravallion, Shaohua, and Sangraula 2007; Badiane 2011; Binswanger-Mkhize 2012).

[6] The link between bio-fuels policies and food prices is complicated and depends on fundamentals in energy and food markets as well as on policies. This complexity has become the topic of intensive research—for example, see de Gorter and Just (2010), de Gorter and Drabik (2012), and Naylor (2012).

[7] Marshall Burke, in a personal communication, has provided a list of why Africa is likely to be more impacted by climate change than other regions, but the most obvious is that "Africa is already hot."

Agriculture also plays an important role in driving climate change, accounting for 14 percent of global greenhouse gas emissions, and this figure more than doubles when deforestation and other land-use changes are included. Forests, thus, are a crucial global natural resource for climate change mitigation. At the global level, the challenge of climate change for the international architecture in agriculture is to continue pushing towards an overarching global climate deal, while contributing to other schemes that support and provide incentives to the absorption and reduction of emissions at the country level. In-country "climate-smart agriculture" adaptation projects and programs now form part of the food policy agenda. The challenge is to design, analyze, and implement these projects and programs.

What should food policy analysts do now?

Despite these changes in the international context, the three basic analytical messages from FPA remain intact: the need for "incentive" food prices to stimulate food production and the rural economy, the use of border prices to measure long-run opportunity costs of production and consumption, and the integration of macro and trade policy into the food policy debate (there was a clear recognition that energy prices were part of macro policy, but perhaps not enough was made of how they connected to food prices directly).

1. The need for price incentives to stimulate production was one of the main themes in FPA, and its importance was reflected by the fact that the chapter on food consumption and nutrition came before the production chapter. Why? This material laid out the analytical underpinnings for the targeted consumer subsidies that would be needed to cope with higher food prices. Because of the overriding concern for poverty reduction in FPA, it argued that policy analysts had to design these subsidy programs and be ready to implement them before the move to higher prices for farmers was initiated. At the time, the higher prices were seen as a policy choice, one that overcame the historical discrimination against agriculture seen in most countries' rural–urban terms of trade, as compared with border prices.

The long-run decline in world food prices from the early 1980s to the mid-2000s gradually called this strategy into question. On the one hand, the decline was welcome because it raised the real purchasing power of the poor. Since much of the decline was stimulated by the Green Revolution and sharply reduced costs of production for rice and wheat, the decline seemed "sustainable," at least in narrow economic terms. The low prices also speeded up the structural transformation, with rapid exit of small farmers from the agricultural sector. This too was "sustainable" in countries with rapidly growing and labor-intensive export industries, as the labor was absorbed while real wages rose. Of course, countries without dynamic macroeconomies had the benefit of low food prices, but real wages stagnated and poverty rose. The dysfunctional structural transformations in Africa (Badiane 2011) and India (Binswangeer-Mkhize 2012) are examples.

The problem was that low food prices in world markets also sent investment signals to governments, donors and research institutions, encouraging them to walk away from the agricultural sector as a crucial source of productivity growth, food security, and poverty reduction. Reduced investments in agriculture and rural infrastructure throughout the 1980s and 1990s resulted in falling rates of productivity growth. Eventually, as students of cobweb cycles understand, growth in food production fell behind growth in food consumption, scarcity re-emerged, and market prices spiraled higher. The world food crisis in late 2007 and early 2008 had its roots directly in this earlier neglect of agricultural investments. Markets were sending the wrong signals to public decision makers, even if private decision makers had no recourse except to heed them (Timmer 1995). The urgent need to find efficient and effective mechanisms to implement food subsidies for the poor, the main point of the chapter on food consumption and nutrition in FPA, seems sadly relevant three decades later. There are more sophisticated approaches now, using conditional cash transfers, improved information technology for screening, and the realization that broader social safety nets might be just as effective as narrower food subsidies. But the food price dilemma has not gone away.

2. Border prices for tradable commodities are the standard measure of opportunity costs for long-run decisions about production and consumption. Although this was beginning to be accepted in principle in the early 1980s, the prevalence of fixed exchange rates and relatively opaque government-to-government trade deals for important food commodities meant that much of the analysis was devoted to figuring out exactly what the long-run border price actually was. This probably seems like arcane history.

There were two problems: knowing what exchange rate to apply, and knowing whether short-run price quotations in world markets reflected longer-run opportunity costs. Much of the project appraisal literature from the late 1970s and early 1980s was devoted to determining the "shadow exchange rate" to be used to calculate effective border prices. Much of Getting Prices Right (Timmer 1986), a "price policy" follow-on to FPA, was devoted to understanding the relevant long-run price trends to use for making public sector investments and to manage domestic price policy interventions.

The first problem has largely been solved, as most countries have adopted reasonably flexible exchange rates that permit the market to indicate the opportunity cost of foreign exchange (although speculative flows of foreign currency make even the market rate somewhat unreliable). Finding the appropriate long-run price signal in the short-run fluctuations still seen in world commodity markets remains elusive. The concern for doing so, clearly articulated in FPA, remains a challenge to food policy analysts (Timmer 2010a). Coping with food price volatility is going to be an even more challenging task in the future as climate change is likely to increase the variability of staple food production.

3. Perhaps the most revolutionary argument in FPA was its insistence that food policy analysis needed to incorporate macroeconomic and trade policy. The argument was not that the policy environment needed for a healthy food system should dictate overall macro and trade policy (although there were certainly some poor agrarian countries where that was likely to be true). The argument was the need for an informed dialogue between food policy analysts and macro policy analysts, with each understanding the stakes on the other side of the table.

Experience over the past three decades has shown the real benefits of this policy dialogue. First, the need for rapid growth in agricultural productivity, with substantial participation by small farmers where they are a significant part of the production structure, is increasingly recognized by macro policymakers as a key element in the overall development strategy. Finance ministers, with their hands on fiscal policy and public investment allocations, central bankers, with their hands on exchange rates and money supplies, and heads of planning agencies, with their hands on strategic approaches and sectoral resource allocations, understand now their own stakes in a healthy rural economy.

In return, food and agricultural planners increasingly understand that real wages in rural areas depend fundamentally on real wages in the urban economy. Real food prices for farmers and consumers are conditioned by the rate of inflation and by exchange rates. Investments in rural infrastructure require budget allocations. Trade policy has direct and indirect effects on rural incentives. The need for a "macro food policy" has never been clearer.

What international regime will be in play?

The components of this macro food policy will be conditioned, as never before, by the international context in which it is formulated. It is both exciting, and troubling, that this international context—the "global food price regime"—is in a greater state of flux, with more uncertainty, than at any time since FPA was being drafted. Institutionally, the current global food policy regime features somewhat more open food markets (although the extent of openness can easily be overstated, especially during crises) and there is virtually no support for public interventions into price formation in global markets, for example, to stabilize or support commodity prices. Thus the international context is now primarily driven by what happens in these markets as a result of basic supply and demand forces, trade policy, and the new connection between food prices and energy prices (mostly driven by policies in rich countries).

Which global food price regime will drive policy formation in the coming quarter century? Will it be the historical path of structural transformation with falling food prices, leading to a "world without agriculture" (Timmer 2009a)? Or will continued financial instability, coupled with the impact of climate change, lead to a new and uncertain path of rising real costs for food with a reversal of structural transformation (Timmer and Akkus 2008)? Management of food policy, and the outlook for sustained poverty reduction, will be radically different depending on which of these global price regimes plays out.

A. The historical pathway of structural transformation with falling food prices

The structural transformation involves four main features:

1. a falling share of agriculture in economic output and employment;

2. a rising share of urban economic activity in industry and modern services;

3. migration of rural workers to urban settings; and

4. a demographic transition in birth and death rates that always leads to a spurt in population growth before a new equilibrium is reached.

These four dimensions of the historical pathway of structural transformation are experienced by all successful developing economies; diversity appears in the various approaches governments have tried to cope with the political pressures generated along that pathway. Finding efficient policy mechanisms that will keep the poor from falling off the pathway altogether has occupied the development profession for decades. There are three key lessons.

First, the structural transformation has been the main pathway out of poverty for all societies, and it depends on rising productivity in both the agricultural and non-agricultural sectors (and the two are connected). The stress on productivity growth in both sectors is important, as agricultural labor can be pushed off of farms into even lower productivity service sector jobs, a perverse form of structural transformation that has generated large pockets of urban poverty, especially in Sub-Saharan Africa and India. Both of these cases have been documented in the Stanford Symposium Series on Global Food Policy and Food Security in the twenty-first century (Badiane 2011; Binswanger-Mkhize 2012). Second, in the early stages, the process of structural transformation widens the gap between labor productivity in the agricultural and non-agricultural sector. This widening puts enormous pressure on rural societies to adjust and modernize. These pressures are then translated into visible and significant policy responses that alter agricultural prices. The agricultural surpluses generated in rich countries because of artificially high prices then cause artificially low prices in world markets and a consequent undervaluation of agriculture in poor countries. This undervaluation over the past several decades, and its attendant reduction in agricultural investments, is a significant factor explaining the world food crisis in 2007/08 and continuing high food prices.

Third, despite the decline in relative importance of the agricultural sector, leading to the "world without agriculture" in rich societies, the process of economic growth and structural transformation requires major investments in the agricultural sector itself. This seeming paradox has complicated (and obfuscated) planning in developing countries as well as donor agencies seeking to speed economic growth and connect the poor to it.

The historical process of structural transformation might seem like a distant hope for the world's poor, who are mostly caught up in eking out a living day by day. There are many things governments can do to give them more immediate hope, such as keeping staple foods cheap and accessible, helping connect rural laborers to urban jobs, and augmenting educational and health services in rural areas. But for poverty-reducing initiatives to be feasible over long periods of time—to be "sustainable" as current development jargon would have it—the indispensable necessity is a growing economy that successfully integrates the rural with urban sectors, and stimulates higher productivity in both. That is, the long-run success of poverty reduction hinges directly on a successful structural transformation. The historical record is very clear on this path.

Coping with the distributional consequences of rapid transformation has turned out to be a major challenge for policymakers over the past half century and the historical record illuminates what works and what does not. Trying to stop the structural transformation simply does not work: and certainly does not work for the poor. Investing in the capacity of the poor to benefit from change, however, does seem to work. Investments in human resources—especially investments in education and health—are the most promising pathways here. Such investment strategies can only be successful if the rest of the economy is doing well, and they typically require significant public sector resources and policy support to enhance rural productivity. These rural investment strategies depend on political processes that are themselves conditioned by the pressures generated by the structural transformation.

A "world without agriculture" would actually make life much easier for development agencies and for politicians in rich countries. "Getting agriculture moving" in poor countries is a complicated, long-run process that requires close, but changing, relationships between the public and private sectors. Donor agencies are not good at this. More problematic, the process of agricultural development requires good economic governance in the countries themselves if it is to work rapidly and efficiently. Aid donors cannot hope to contribute good governance themselves—and may well impede it.

The strong historical tendency toward a widening of income differences between rural and urban economies during the initial stages of the structural transformation is now extending much further into the development process. Consequently, with little prospect of reaching quickly the turning point, where farm and non-farm productivity and incomes begin to converge, many poor countries are turning to agricultural protection and farm subsidies sooner rather than later in their development process. The tendency of these actions to hurt the poor is then compounded, because there are so many more rural poor in these early stages.

B. Climate change, bio-fuels, rising food prices, and the potential to reverse the structural transformation

Will climate change lead to a reversal of long-run downward trends in real prices of agricultural commodities? This reversal would be driven by demand for bio-fuels and by the impact of climate change on agricultural productivity—but it would also reverse the steady movement to higher income levels of the turning point in convergence of labor productivity in rural and urban areas during the structural transformation. If so, the short-run impact on the poor is almost certain to be negative, but the higher real returns promised to commodity producers, without agricultural protection, could stimulate the broad array of rural investments needed to generate productivity increases in rural areas, raise real wages, and be the long-run pathway out of rural poverty. Climate change might actually make many farmers better off.

Bio-fuels and food policy

Bio-fuels are not new. Although coal was known in China in pre-historic times, and was traded in England as early as the thirteenth century, it was not used widely for industrial purposes until the seventeenth century. Until then, bio-fuels were virtually the only source of energy for human economic activities, and for many poor people they remain so today. But the widespread use of fossil fuels since the Industrial Revolution has provided a huge subsidy to modern economic activities—because coal and later petroleum were so cheap—a subsidy which seems to be nearing an end.

What will be the role of bio-fuels going forward, and what will be the impact on agriculture? In the extreme, the demand for bio-fuels in rich countries to power their automobiles has the potential to raise the price of basic agricultural commodities to such a level that the entire structural transformation could be reversed. If so, the growing use of bio-fuels has two alternative futures: it could spell impoverishment for much of the world's population because of the resulting high food prices, or it could spell dynamism for rural economies and the eventual end of rural poverty. Which future turns out to be the case depends fundamentally on the location, technology, economics, and politics of bio-fuel production.

The potential devastating effects of bio-fuels are easy to conceptualize (Naylor 2012). The income elasticity of demand for starchy staples (cereals and root crops for direct human consumption) is less than 0.2 on average, and falling with higher incomes—it is already negative in much of Asia. Adding in the indirect demand from grain-fed livestock products brings the average income elasticity to about 0.5, and this is holding steady in the face of rapid economic growth in India and China. Potential supply growth seems capable of managing this growth in demand.

But the demand for bio-fuels is almost insatiable in relation to the base of production of staple foods (a point emphasized on p. 185 of FPA). The income elasticity of demand for liquid fuels for automobile and truck fleets, not to mention power generation, is greater than one in developing countries. The average for the world is rising as middle class consumers in China, India and beyond seek to graduate from bicycles to motorbikes to automobiles. One simple calculation shows the dimension of the problem: if all the corn produced in the United States were used for ethanol to fuel automobiles, it would replace just 15 percent of current gasoline consumption in the United States. Something has to give.

If this were a market-driven process, it is easy to see what will give. High grain prices will make ethanol production uneconomic, driving down the demand (and returns on investments in ethanol processing plants). Greater profitability of grain production will stimulate a supply response, although this may take several years if improved technologies are needed. Grain prices will reach a new equilibrium, with demand from the bio-fuel industry having only a modest impact.

This is not the scenario most analysts see. Instead, political mandates to expand bio-fuel production in many countries will continue to drive investments in processing facilities and the need to keep these profitable in the face of high raw material prices will require large public subsidies. Rich countries will be able to afford these more easily than poor countries, so a combination of inelastic demand for fuel and a willingness to pay large subsidies will keep grain prices very high (Naylor 2012; de Gorter and Just 2010).

If this scenario plays out, what are the consequences for economic growth and poverty reductions in developing countries? Not surprisingly, the answer depends on the role of agriculture in individual countries, the pattern of commodity production and the distribution of rural assets, especially land. It is certainly possible to see circumstances where small farmers respond to higher grain prices by increasing output and reaping higher incomes. These incomes might be spent in the local, rural non-farm economy, stimulating investments and raising wages for non-farm workers. In such environments, higher grain prices could stimulate an upward spiral of prosperity.

An alternative scenario seems more likely however, partly because the role of small farmers has been under so much pressure in the past several decades. If only large farmers are able to reap the benefits of higher grain prices, and their profits do not stimulate a dynamic rural economy, a downward spiral can start for the poor. High food prices cut their food intake, children are sent to work instead of school and an intergenerational poverty trap develops. If the poor are numerous enough, the entire economy is threatened, and the structural transformation comes to a halt. The share of agriculture in both employment and GDP starts to rise, and this reversal condemns future generations to lower living standards. There will be much more "structural" poverty, and countries determined to cope with it will find themselves supporting expensive and long-term safety nets for the poor.

A reversal of the structural transformation as the regular path to economic development and reduced poverty will be a historical event, countering the patterns generated by market forces over the past several centuries. Such an event is likely to have stark political consequences, as populations do not face the sustained prospect of lower living standards with equanimity. It is possible, of course, that new technologies will come on-stream and lower energy costs across the board and thus allow the bio-fuel dilemma to disappear quietly. But it looks like a rocky couple of decades before that happens.

A food policy response to climate change

The bio-fuel challenge to food policy analysts stems from efforts to mitigate climate change. Equally challenging will be efforts to adapt agriculture to the dual effects of climate change—higher temperatures and greater variability in rainfall. In their summary to the chapter on "Food Security and Adaptation to Climate Change: What Do We Know?" Burke and Lobell make the following observations:

> The rapid pace of climate change and its anticipated large negative effects on many agricultural systems suggest a broad and pressing need for adaptation. For farming households, the nature of these responses will depend on their recognition that climate is changing and their ability to adjust their behavior in response, perhaps through altering farm management practices or diversifying into off-farm income-generating activities. Such responses must happen in the context of climate variability, which can obscure longer-run climate trends and make more risky the adoption of various adaptation measures. Further contributing to the difficulties is the limited choice set already faced by many food insecure households, which is often the result of high productivity risk, lack of access to insurance and credit, and/or limited connection to functioning input and output markets. As a result, broader public and private investments will almost certainly be needed to help poor households adapt to climate change. These could include direct investments in the productivity of agriculture, such as the development of improved crop varieties better suited to new climates, investments aimed at improving the physical and market infrastructure that typically underpin functioning economies, or investments that bolster the social safety nets that help poor households maintain their welfare in the face of a livelihood shock. While the optimal composition of investments will vary by country, scientific research can contribute important information concerning where climate change will hit hardest, how agricultural systems are likely to respond, and what particular investments in adaptation could yield high returns. (Burke and Lobell 2010: 151, 152)

A particularly insightful example of the kind of food policy analysis that will be needed to cope with climate change grows out of the experience in Indonesia, where weather events, mostly El Nino-Southern Oscillation (ENSO) dynamics, are particularly well studied[8]. The external dynamics provide a strong case for a causal link from El Nino to rice production and local food security, and via trade changes, to global rice prices.

These ENSO effects on Indonesia's national and regional rice production and on world rice prices have been studied extensively by Stanford University scientists and their colleagues (Falcon, et al. 2004; Naylor and Mastrandrea 2009). Using the August sea surface temperature anomaly (SSTA) to gauge climate variability, their work shows that each degree Celsius change in the August SSTA produces a 1.32 million metric ton effect on rice output and a $21 per metric ton change in the world price for lower quality rice. These relationships offer policymakers a forward looking tool to prepare for threats to local food security, as emphasized in the final report to the National Science Foundation detailing what was learned from a research project on this topic:

> Agricultural production in Indonesia is strongly influenced by the annual cycle of precipitation and the year-to-year variations in the annual cycle of precipitation caused by El Niño-Southern Oscillation (ENSO) dynamics. The combined forces of ENSO and global warming are likely to have dramatic, and currently unforeseen, effects on agriculture production and food security in Indonesia and other tropical countries. This project combined general circulation model (GCM) experiments and empirical downscaling models (EDMs) to assess the influence of global warming on the annual cycle, and on ENSO-induced changes in precipitation and agricultural production in Indonesia. A risk assessment framework was then developed to evaluate how climate-related uncertainty and probable agricultural outcomes derived from the downscaling model can be used in policy decision-making processes. The models focused on rice, the country's primary food staple. ...
>
> Over the longer-term, our Bayesian approach could be used to help Indonesian policymakers anticipate ENSO impacts in a warmer world. Given the projections in our study of a significant change in the annual cycle of precipitation in the region, policymakers could use updated climate information for adaptation; that is, they might want to invest in water storage facilities (reservoirs and linked irrigation systems) to take advantage of periods of more intense rainfall and cover longer dry periods. They also might want to invest in drought tolerant crops, or provide incentives for alterations in cropping systems that match both climate conditions and market demand.
>
> In this particular case, the Bayesian null hypothesis would be a change in the annual cycle of precipitation that affects crop production, food availabilities, and incomes throughout the year. The prior would be established on the basis of the observed annual cycle going back in time for decades, and this prior would be updated with new information as the years progressed. The likelihood of the null hypothesis being true could thus increase over time as more information became available on the pattern of rainfall over the course of the year. This analysis is very different from the Bayesian analysis of El Niño events described above for the short term, because a long-run change in the climate's mean state has not yet been fully established (beyond historical patterns of variability). (Naylor et al. 2009)

[8] It somehow seems appropriate that Indonesia should be a leading example of food policy analysis of climate change impacts because the country also served as the learning and teaching foundation for Food Policy Analysis, as is described in the Preface to FPA (see pages ix-x).

In pulling together their final thoughts on the impact of climate change on food availability, food access, and food utilization—the three main factors that determine food security—Lobell and Burke make the following observation:

> ...one thing appears almost certainly true in the twenty-first century; if agriculture and food security are to thrive, they will have to do so in a constantly warming world. The level of climate stability that has been experienced since the dawn of agriculture is a thing of the past; the future will be one of constant change. This need not spell disaster for food security, but we would be wise not to underestimate the enormity of the challenge at hand. (Lobell and Burke 2010)

Food policy analysis that understands this challenge and offers insights into how best to cope with it will be a key driver of how successfully society adapts to climate change.

Reflections on food policy analysis in a rapidly changing world

The historical evolution of food policy analysis described in this paper raises several questions going forward: who will do the analysis and where will they be trained; what is the appropriate institutional base for food policy analysts; and why do this difficult analysis if "politics is in command?"

The human capital investment needed to train skilled food policy analysts is substantial and the educational institutions capable of providing the training are hard to find. A successful food policy analyst needs an unusual blend of technical skills, mostly economic, and a broad vision of how food systems interact and evolve over time. University Ph.D. programs have basically stopped doing this kind of training. Economics programs, for example, increasingly focus on micro economic decision making that needs to be understood through careful experimental design of the data needed for analysis. Some extraordinarily smart students have come out of these programs with field experience in rural settings, and their journal articles are technical gems. But it is rare for these students to be trained in the macroeconomics of growth and development, much less economic history. Almost none understand climate models or even the basic elements of energy and nutrient flows. Such students have little intuition about how complex food systems function and change. Undergraduates seeking graduate programs to train them as food policy analysts have nowhere to go.

The failure of academic programs to provide coherent training in food policy analysis is partly due to the lack of clear career tracks for such analysts. Just where are the jobs? What institutional base provides the best opportunities for food policy analysts to do good work and be effective advocates for sound policies and programs? The historical record is quite fuzzy, as successful food policy units have functioned in planning agencies, food logistics agencies, trade and commerce ministries, ministries of health, even ministries of agriculture. But there is no clear set of lessons on which institutional base provides the best incentives for high quality analysis that is effectively plugged into the policy process. Perhaps serendipity and leadership are the key variables in such success.

Finally, there are a set of questions that revolve around the political economy of food policy. When "politics is in command," which seems to be the normal state of affairs for most developing countries (at least in the short run), how do efficiency issues stay on the agenda?

When "markets are in command," which seems to be the main policy advice from the donor community to poor countries, how do distributional and welfare issues stay on the agenda (that is, how do countries develop the capacity to "push back" against donor advice that will drive them out of office)? How can "markets" and "politics" together win democratic elections? More broadly, how do we educate policymakers as well as analysts? In democratic societies it would seem to require educating citizens so that they could be informed voters. Doing so will require a much deeper, behavioral understanding of how both citizens and policymakers make decisions (Timmer 2012). Research in this arena is just getting underway.

References

Badiane, Ousmane. 2011. "Agriculture and Structural Transformation in Africa." Stanford Symposium Series on Global Food Policy and Food Security in the 21st Century, April 7, Stanford University.

Binswanger-Mkhize, Hans P. 2012. "India 1960–2010: Structural Change, the Rural Non-farm Sector, and the Prospects for Agriculture." Stanford Symposium Series on Global Food Policy and Food Security in the 21st Century, May 10, Stanford University.

Burke, Marshall, and David Lobell. 2010. "Food Security and Adaptation to Climate Change: What Do We Know?" In *Climate Change and Food Security: Adapting Agriculture to a Warmer World*. Advances in Global Change Research 37, edited by David Lobell and Marshall Burke, 133-53. B. V. Heidelberg, London and New York: Springer.

De Gorter, Harry, and Dusan Drabik. 2012. "The Effect of Biofuel Policies on Food Grain Commodity Prices." *Biofuels* 3 (1): 21-24.

De Gorter, Harry, and David R. Just. 2010. "The Social Costs and Benefits of Biofuels: The Intersection of Environmental, Energy and Agricultural Policy." *Applied Economic Perspectives and Policy* 32 (1): 4-32.

Falcon, Walter P., Rosamond L. Naylor, Whitney L. Smith, Marshall B. Burke, and Ellen B. McCullough. 2004. "Using Climate Models to Improve Indonesian Food Security." *Bulletin of Indonesian Economic Studies* 40 (3): 357-79.

Lobell, D., and M. Burke, eds. 2010. *Climate Change and Food Security: Adapting Agriculture to a Warmer World*. Advances in Global Change Research 37. B. V. Heidelberg, London and New York: Springer.

Naylor, R. 2012. "Biofuels, Rural Development, and the Changing Nature of Agricultural Demand." Stanford Symposium Series on Global Food Policy and Food Security in the 21st Century. April 11, Stanford University.

Naylor, R., D. Battisti, D. Vimont, and W. Falcon. 2009. "Agricultural Decision-Making in Indonesia with ENSO Variability: Integrating Climate Science, Risk Assessment, and Policy Analysis." Final Report, NSF Award ID: 0433679 (Project start date: 10/02/04). July, Stanford University.

Naylor, R., and M. Mastrandrea. 2010. "Coping with Climate Risks in Indonesian Rice Agriculture: A Policy Perspective." *In Uncertainty and Environmental Decision Making. Handbook of Research and Best Practice*, edited by J.A. Filer, and A. Haurie, 127-51. Springer International Series in Operations Research and Management Science. New York: Springer.

Ravallion, M., C. Shaohua, and P. Sangraula. 2007. "New Evidence on the Urbanization of Global Poverty." Policy Research Working Paper 4199, April. Washington, DC: The World Bank.

Reardon, T., and C.P. Timmer. 2012. "The Economics of the Food System Revolution." *Annual Review of Resource Economics* 4: 14.1-14.40.

Streeten, P. 1982. *First Things First: Meeting Basic Human Needs*. London: Oxford University Press.

Timmer, C.P. 1986. *Getting Prices Right: The Scope and Limits of Agricultural Price Policy*. Ithaca: Cornell University Press.

Timmer, C.P. 1995. "Getting Agriculture Moving: Do Markets Provide the Right Signals?" *Food Policy* 20 (5): 455-72.

Timmer, C.P. 2009a. "A World without Agriculture: The Structural Transformation in Historical Perspective." Wendt Distinguished Lecture. Washington, DC: American Enterprise Institute.

Timmer, C.P. 2009b. "Do Supermarkets Change the Food Policy Agenda?" *World Development*, Special Issue on "Agrifood Industry Transformation and Small Farmers in Developing Countries," guest eds T. Reardon, C.B. Barrett, J.A. Berdegué, and J.F.M. Swinnen 37 (11): 1812-19.

Timmer, C.P. 2010a. "Reflections on Food Crises Past." *Food Policy* 35 (1): 1-11.

Timmer, C.P. 2010b. "International Best Practice in Food Policy: Reflections on Food Policy Analysis." *Asian Journal of Agriculture and Development* 7 (1): 1-10.

Timmer, C.P. 2012. "Behavioral Dimensions of Food Security." Proceedings of the National Academy of Sciences (*Agricultural Development and Nutrition Security Special Feature*), 109 (31): 12355-20.

Timmer, C.P., and S. Akkus. 2008. "The Structural Transformation as a Pathway out of Poverty: Analytics, Empirics and Politics." Working Paper 150. Washington, DC: Center for Global Development.

Timmer, C.P., W.P. Falcon, and S.R. Pearson. 1983. *Food Policy Analysis*. Baltimore, MD: Johns Hopkins University Press for the World Bank.

World Bank. 1993. *The East Asian Miracle: Economic Growth and Public Policy*. New York: Oxford University Press.

Making Food Systems Nutrition-sensitive: an Economic Policy Perspective

Per Pinstrup-Andersen[1]

The triple burden of malnutrition, i.e. lack of access to sufficient dietary energy, micronutrient deficiencies and overweight and obesity, causes widespread human misery, low labor productivity and large economic losses to individuals and societies. While most efforts to improve nutrition have focused on direct interventions, the results have been disappointing. Opportunities for nutrition improvements through changes in the food system are large and largely ignored. Merely producing more food does not assure better nutrition. Most malnutrition, particularly overweight and obesity but also much of the existing energy and nutrient deficiencies, occurs amidst plenty of food at the national or global levels. Thus, assuming that the food system's only role in improving nutrition is to produce more food is a fallacy. Food policy should pursue improved nutrition along with other food system goals, and trade-offs among the various goals should be addressed. The pathways between food systems and nutrition, including those operating through food availability, incomes, food prices, gender-specific time allocation, should be identified and household behavior should be fully understood.

Keywords: malnutrition, food system-nutrition pathways, policy interventions

That food systems affect human nutrition should be obvious to all of us. Without food, we perish. But the nutrition effect of a food system depends on its characteristics and the environment within which it operates and the impact on nutrition may be influenced by policy interventions. Whether an outcome of policy interventions or not, changes in a food system may improve nutrition, e.g., eliminating iron deficiencies, or the nutritional status may deteriorate, e.g., causing excessive intake of dietary energy resulting in obesity and associated diabetes. Good nutrition is very important for individuals and societies and one might imagine that food systems would be guided by health and nutrition goals. That is not usually the case. Food systems are guided by the behavior of agents in the system pursuing economic goals and when they conflict with health and nutrition goals, the former usually dominates. This is not a value judgment that one set of goals is "better" than another but simply an observation that market-based economies operate on the basis of supply and demand and not on needs and compassion.

The question addressed in this article is which public policy interventions might make economic goals compatible with nutrition goals, that is, reducing or removing the above-mentioned conflict. In other words, what could governments do to make food systems more nutrition-sensitive? On the surface, the answer may appear straight forward: produce the food people need and

[1] H. E. Babcock Professor of Food, Nutrition and Public Policy, Professor of Applied Economics, Cornell University, Ithaca, New York and Adjunct Professor, University of Copenhagen, Copenhagen, Denmark.

make sure they eat it. In reality, it is extremely complicated. Even centrally planned command economies that tried or at least pretended to try, have failed. In order to identify the possible policy interventions, it is essential to understand the pathways through which food systems may affect nutrition and to pin point the main factors in each pathway that cause economic and nutrition goals to differ. These factors may be external to the food system or they may be integrated into the system. Policy interventions may aim to change the socioeconomic environment within which food systems operate or they may focus on changing system-specific physical and behavioral factors.

One might expect that overall economic welfare would be maximized in a market economy's food system if every system agent, including farmers, traders, and consumers, would maximize his/her economic welfare. But even in such a situation, the net positive nutrition effect is unlikely to be maximized in the absence of government intervention. The physical and socioeconomic environments may not be conducive to the production, trade, and consumption of the foods needed to assure good nutrition and the behavior of farmers, processors, consumers, and other food system agents may seek goals other than good nutrition.

Increasing and more volatile food prices since 2007 and widespread concerns about future food supplies and unsustainable management of natural resources have drawn the attention of policymakers towards the world food situation. Although most recent policy responses have been of a short-run nature, e.g., fertilizer subsidies, a consensus is developing—at least rhetorically—among national policymakers and international organizations that investments in long-term agricultural development, such as agricultural research, must be increased. Thus, members of the G8 and G20 have committed large increases in international economic support for such investments and some developing countries such as Ethiopia and Ghana are planning large new investments. While most of these recent initiatives focus on expanded food supplies, it is now generally understood that just making more food available will not assure better food security, nutrition and health at the household and individual levels (Herforth, Jones, and Pinstrup-Andersen 2012; Pinstrup-Andersen 2012a; Hawkes and Ruel 2006). The International Obesity Task Force suggests a three-pronged strategy: include nutritional criteria in agricultural policies, undertake health impact assessment of such policies, and provide support for agricultural programs aimed at meeting World Health Organization (WHO)'s dietary guidelines (Hawkes 2007). It matters for health and nutrition how the increasing food supply is brought about, of what it consists and what happens to it in the food system.

This is not a new argument (Pinstrup-Andersen, de Londono, and Hoover 1976; Pinstrup-Andersen 1981; WHO 2004), but its application in the design and implementation of food system policies has been very limited. That is still the case. The rhetoric has gained prominence but very little action has followed. The recently established Scaling-up Nutrition (SUN) Framework calls for action to address malnutrition through agriculture and other sectors. Several recent documents by the Department for International Development (DFID), the European Commission, United States Agency for International Development's Feed the Future Guide and World Vision focus on how to strengthen the nutrition effects of agricultural development projects and policies (Herforth 2012; SUN

Framework 2010). An international conference hosted by IFPRI on "Leveraging Agriculture for Improving Nutrition and Health" in 2011 discussed how best to proceed and Food and Agriculture Organization (FAO) and WHO are focusing the upcoming International Conference on Nutrition on the same topic.

The increasing attention to the link between the food system and human nutrition is also an outcome of the failure of past direct nutrition interventions to significantly reduce the widespread nutritional deficiencies as well as the rapidly increasing prevalence of overweight, obesity, and resulting chronic diseases (Hawkes et al. 2012a; Nugent 2011). Nutrition goals are frequently mentioned in plans and strategies for the food system, but they are usually not taken into account in the actual execution of the plans.

The next section discusses the most important pathways and suggests policy interventions that may make the food system more nutrition-sensitive, then follows brief sections about policy implementation and the available evidence and knowledge gaps. The article ends with a brief concluding section. A list of policy interventions that may be considered to make the food system more nutrition-sensitive is shown in the appendix.

The food system-nutrition pathways and policy interventions

Nutrition may be affected by food systems through multiple pathways. As a starting point it may be useful to visualize food systems in an evolutionary manner beginning with subsistence farm households producing food only for own consumption (let us call that stage 1). The next stage (stage 2) would be production for sale for direct consumption, followed by the production of raw materials (commodities) for a food processing industry (stage 3) and ending with the production of ingredients which will be used along with synthetic ingredients by the processing industry to produce the food offered to consumers (stage 4). In reality, the four stages exist today as part of a continuum and have somewhat different pathways.

Interventions to improve nutrition in stage 1 should be focused on changing production by changing either the physical and socioeconomic environment or household behavior. Factors such as access to improved crop varieties, fertilizers, and other inputs; gender-specific intra-household labor and time demand as well as food allocation among household members; and lack of knowledge related to production and nutrition may be responsive to policy interventions. As further discussed below, policy interventions to help assure crop diversity in production and relief of women's time demand are likely to be particularly important. Although households in stage 1 do not produce food for sale, most are likely to earn income from the sale of non-foods or off-farm employment. Thus, food may be purchased to complement own production. That brings us into stage 2 in which households, whether they produce food or not, confront a longer pathway in which relative prices, incomes, the structure of the post-harvest supply chain, and gender-specific time demand take on increasing importance.

The diet transition from staples to non-staple foods begins in stage 2 and gains speed in stage 3. Although the diet transition differs among countries, the diet transition in China provides a rough illustration of a transition likely to take place in a country with economic growth (Figures 1 and 2). It also illustrates the different diet compositions in countries at different income levels. The diet up to 1980–81 consisted primarily of grains and vegetables. Energy and nutrient deficiencies were widespread. This is characteristic of low-income countries, although roots and tubers may be more important in some countries. By 1990, the consumption of vegetable oil and foods of animal origin had increased significantly while the consumption of cereals and vegetables stayed constant, thus increasing calorie intake, characteristic of many lower middle-income countries. Poverty and energy deficiencies decreased dramatically due to income growth, changing agricultural policies and related rural development. As the consumption of vegetable oil and foods of animal origin jumped to new highs, grain and vegetable consumption dropped. The prevalence of overweight and obesity increased, a common development for middle-to-high income countries. Projections are that the trend towards excessive intake of dietary energy, a higher prevalence of obesity and a larger burden of chronic diseases, will continue for the foreseeable future in China and globally. An understanding of where a particular country or community is in the diet transition is important to identify the most appropriate policy interventions.

The importance of the food processing industry has increased dramatically during the recent past and processed foods occupy a rapidly increasing share of the diet even in low- and middle-income countries (stages 3 and 4). This transition from direct consumption of farm-produced food to processed foods relegating farmers to producers of raw materials and ingredients for processing is undoubtedly the most important issue linking food systems to nutrition and health. It is also likely to be the most important pathway for future nutrition-sensitive policy intervention. Yet, most past and current research and debate about how to make the food system more nutrition-sensitive is focused on agriculture and not the post-harvest value chain where the greatest opportunities exist for avoiding harmful nutrition effects and enhancing positive ones. This does not mean that policy interventions for pathways in stages one and two should be ignored. The majority of the world's poor people live in rural areas and the food consumption would be best characterized as belonging to stages 1 and 2. However, processed foods are rapidly expanding their importance in the diets of both rural and urban poor. This is so partly because of aggressive advertising and promotion resulting from globalization and widespread access to information and communications technology and partly due to rapid changes in the food retail sector, including the spread of supermarkets. In response to this development and in opposition to the transport of food over long distances and the related changes in the agricultural sector towards large-scale, technological advanced production of raw materials to the processing industry, movements promoting the consumption of locally and/organically produced food are gaining ground, particularly in high-income countries. The potential nutrition implications of these movements are discussed below.

Several pathways through which food system interventions can affect nutrition have been suggested in recent literature (Arimond et al. 2011; Gillespie and Kadiyala 2012; The World Bank 2007; Jones 2011; Hoddinott 2012). These authors seem to agree that production for own consumption, incomes, prices, gender-specific time allocation, food availability (quantity and quality), and household behavior provide important links between the food system and household access to food and nutrition. They clearly reject the commonly held no-

Figure 1. Per Capita Annual Consumption of Selected Food Groups by Chinese Rural Households (Index, 2009=100)

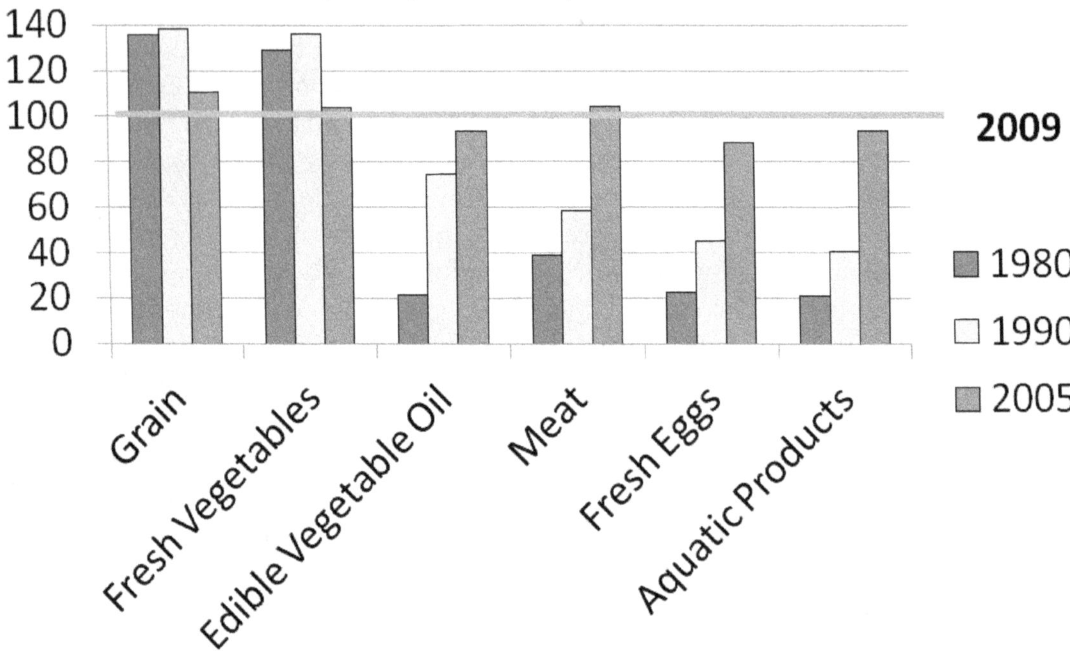

Source: NBS China Statistical Year Book, 1987 and 2010.

Figure 2. Per Capita Annual Consumption of Selected Food Groups by Chinese Urban Households (Index, 2009=100)

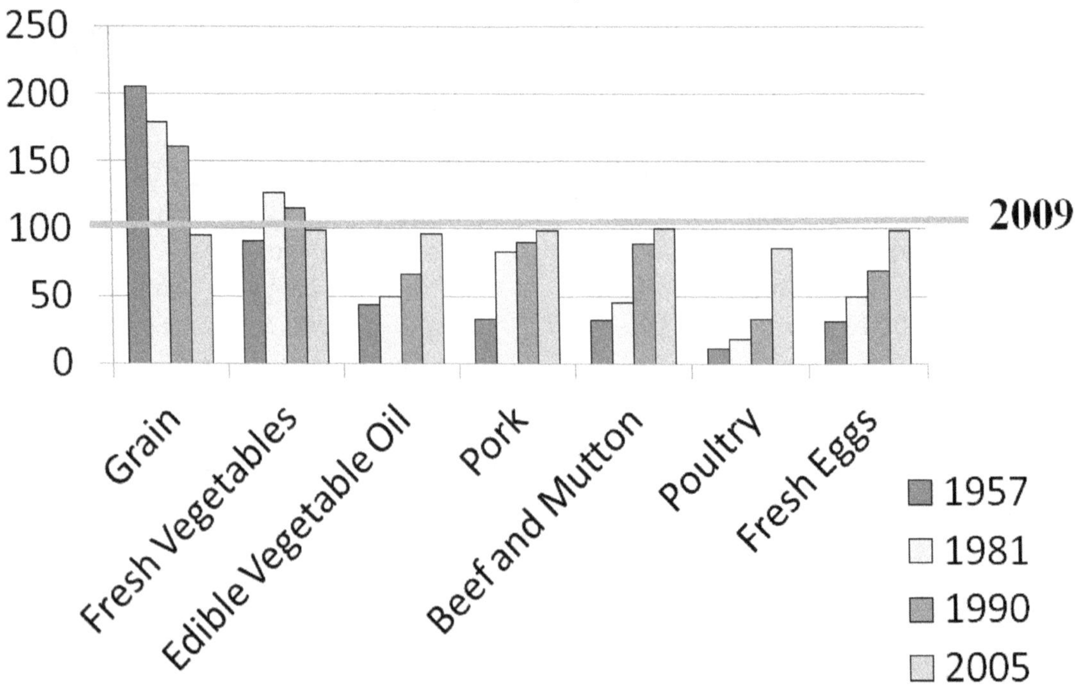

Source: NBS China Statistical Year Book, 1987 and 2010.

tion that the quantity of food produced is the food system's sole link to human nutrition. The effect of food system interventions such as the promotion of export crop production may increase household incomes and household food security (measured in dietary energy) without having any effect on child nutrition (Kennedy, Bouis, and von Braun 1992; von Braun and Kennedy 1994). Such an outcome would be expected where diarrhea or other infectious diseases, or low-quality diets rather than lack of food quantity, are the most limiting factors in efforts to improve child nutrition. Clean water, good sanitation and hygiene, and care are important aspects of good nutrition.

The six factors mentioned above are key components of the pathways through which food systems may affect nutrition. A generic pathway, likely to be relevant for all four stages, is shown in Figure 3. With no exception, each of the factors shown in Figure 3 may be influenced by policies and projects which in turn may influence nutrition.

Food availability

The availability of food is necessary but not sufficient to assure food security and good nutrition. Availability depends on the behavior of the private sector, including farmers, traders and processors, and government policies. For example, trade liberalization may increase the availability of imported foods with undesirable characteristics such as processed foods with a high content of fats and sweeteners. Investments in research and processing by the private sector may develop new products beneficial or harmful to nutrition. Availability of meat, dairy products, fruits, and vegetables may reduce micronutrient deficiencies while availability of fats, oils, sugar, sweeteners, and energy-dense, nutrient-poor foods may contribute to overweight, obesity, chronic diseases as well as nutrient deficiencies. A high degree of diversity in the food supply, whether from own production or from the market, is key to facilitate consumption diversity and better nutrition.

Research and policy interventions to promote the production, marketing, and consumption of so-called "orphan crops" provide opportunities for enhancing consumption diversity, and reducing micronutrient deficiencies, on semi-subsistence farms, and local markets where the diet may consist of one or two basic staples. The diet diversity may also be enhanced through the promotion of kitchen gardens and increasing consumption of animal products. In locations where water resources are available, aquaculture may improve diet diversity through fish and seafood consumption and income-generating sales. The nutrition value of foods may be improved by industrial fortification and biofortification. However, industrial fortification increases the price of food and would not be relevant for food that does not pass through processing. Thus, it would not work for families that consume unprocessed foods. Biofortification depends on farmers' adoption of the fortified seed, and consumers' acceptance, ability, and willingness to pay a higher price, if necessary.

Research and technological change in agriculture deserve much credit for the current ample food supply and increase in calorie consumption. Modern scientific methods, including that based on molecular biology together with technological innovations in information and communication technology, offer great opportunities for meeting future food demand at reasonable prices. However, to achieve sustainable food security and improved health and nutrition, it should be focused on productivity increase of a diverse portfolio of foods with a bias towards smallholders and reduced

Figure 3. A Simplified Conceptual Framework Linking Food Availability, Food Security, Health and Nutrition.

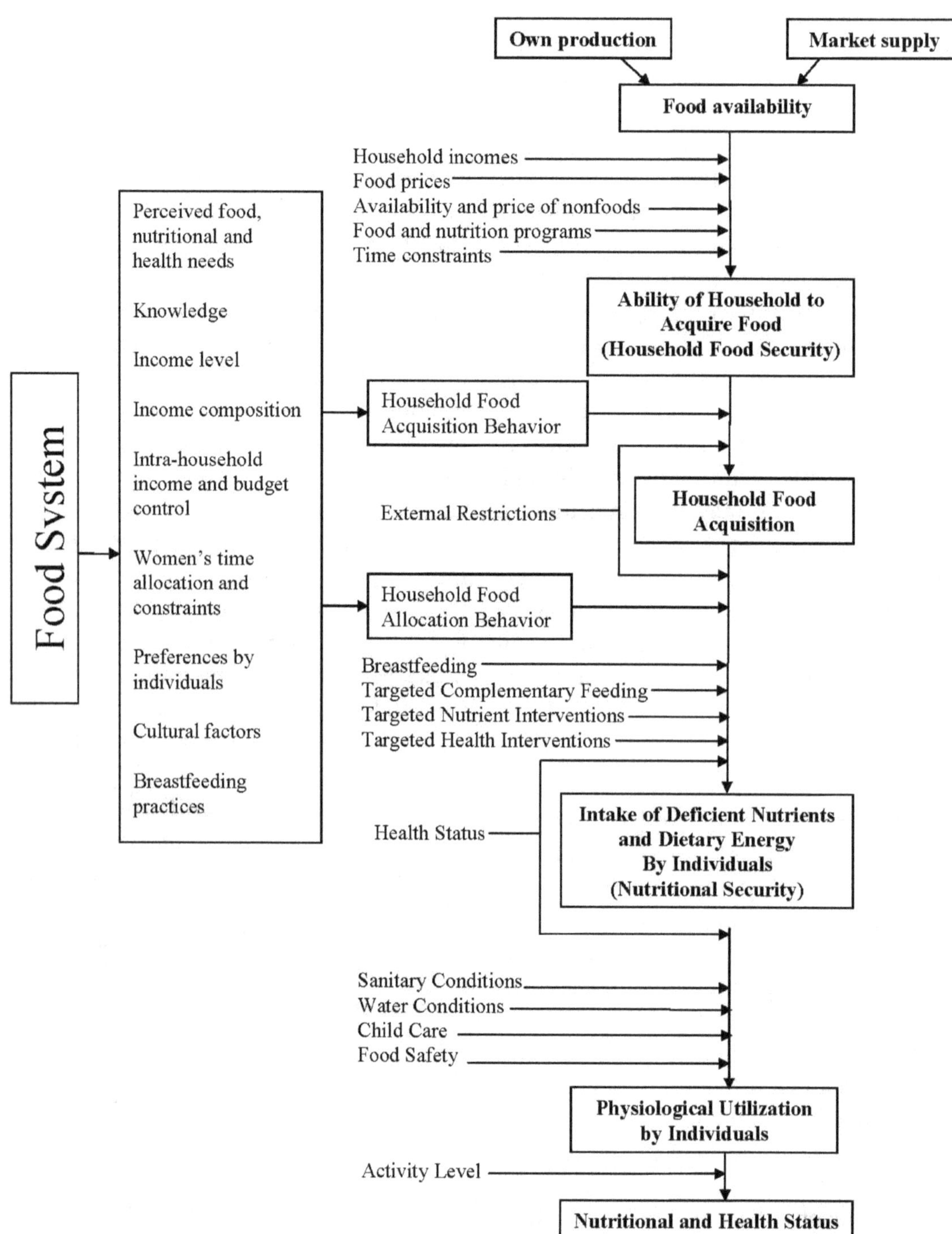

Source: Pinstrup-Andersen and Watson (2011).

unit-costs of production and marketing. Research to improve the nutritional quality of food through biofortification, post-harvest fortification and improved processing, storage, and transportation, should be expanded. A shift from processing to produce foods with a high content of refined sugar, sweeteners, fats, and oils to foods with a high content of micronutrients could be promoted through taxes on sugar, sweeteners, fats, and oils; government financial support of fortification; research and technology development for nutrient-dense foods such as fruits and vegetables; and educational and promotional programs to alter consumer demand. Biofortification of sweet potato has yielded good nutrition results (Low et al. 2007) and research currently under way to enhance the content of vit-A, iron, and zinc in several other staple crops look promising (Bouis et al. 2011).

Biofuel production based on maize, soybeans, rapeseed, jatropha, and oil palm competes with food production for land and water resources while generating incomes for producers. The profitability of biofuel production is closely related to government policies and oil prices and future fluctuations in the latter are likely to cause food price fluctuations. Although estimates vary, it appears that the expansion of biofuel production contributed significantly to the food price increases during 2007–08 (Rausser and de Gorter, forthcoming). The nutrition impact will depend on the extent of price increase and the proportion of the income increase captured by smallholder farmers with malnourished members.

International land grabbing, i.e., acquiring control over land by multinational corporations or foreign government agencies through agreements with governments in countries where the land is found, may increase agricultural production of foods and non-foods including raw material for biofuel. It may also contribute to economic growth in the communities where the land is located. Employment of landless labor and farmers who previously cultivated the land may reduce rural poverty and improve food security and nutrition. If the additional food produced is sold in the country where it is produced, it may lower food prices for the benefit for net buyers while harming net sellers. Unfortunately, much land grabbing pushes smallholder families off their land while providing little or no alternative sources of income. The number of farmers and landless workers who gain employment is small and the foods and non-foods produced are usually exported (Robertson and Pinstrup-Andersen 2010; Deininger and Byerlee 2011; German, Schoneveld, and Mwangi 2011; Oxfam 2011; Cotula et al. 2009). While international guidelines for land grabbing exist, there is no indication they are being followed (World Bank 2010; Robertson and Pinstrup-Andersen 2010). Regulatory policies are urgently needed to protect the rural poor from adverse effects of the land grabbing agreements entered into by several developing country governments with little or no consultation with the affected rural poor.

Climate change and unsustainable management of natural resources make the achievement of good nutrition difficult. Extreme weather events cause fluctuations in food production and food prices and increasing temperature and changing rainfall patterns make rain-fed agriculture in tropical areas more risky and less productive. Policies to assist farmers to adapt to climate change and related extreme weather events are important means to protect the nutrition of the rural poor, notably those in the lowest-income countries in the tropics (Pinstrup-Andersen and Watson 2011).

In addition to the above-mentioned processing and fortification, the nutritional quality and safety of foods may be improved or deteriorated by action or lack of action in storage, transportation, and other food system activities. Waste and losses in the food supply chain are large. Gustavsson et al. (2011) estimate that 1.3 billion tons of food are lost or wasted annually. That corresponds to the calorie needs of 2–3 billion people, or roughly equivalent to the projected population increase between now and 2050. Adding pre-harvest production lost to plant and animal diseases and pest attacks in farmers' fields, the large opportunities for expanding the food available for actual consumption become obvious.

The global population is expected to grow to about 9 billion by 2050 and by another 1–2 billion before stabilizing around the end of the century. Population growth together with increasing incomes and the dietary change towards more animal sourced food is expected to increase food demand by 60% during the next 35 years, corresponding to about 1.4% accumulated annual increase. This is doable without increasing real food prices if appropriate policies are implemented (Pinstrup-Andersen 2012b). From a nutritional perspective, the composition of the food produced and who produces it are critically important. Large-scale capital intensive mono-crop production of the kind expected to result from land grabbing exported to middle-income countries may meet production goals but at the expense of food security and nutrition. Policy interventions are needed to guide private investment towards the production of a diverse portfolio of foods that generates income and food security in households with malnourished members and lower unit-costs of production and food prices. While food availability is necessary for good nutrition, changes in food availability will not have any impact on nutrition unless the actual or potentially malnourished people have access. As shown in Figure 3, access, or the ability of households to acquire the food available, is influenced by incomes, own production, food prices, availability and prices of nonfoods, and social safety nets. These factors and the related behavioral and policy aspects are discussed next.

Incomes

Changes in the food system may affect incomes of the actual or potentially malnourished people in several ways. Firstly, research and technology may generate an economic surplus by improving productivity of land, water, or labor, not only in agriculture but also in other parts of the food system. Depending on relative demand and supply elasticities and market structure, conduct, and performance, the surplus may result in higher incomes (in cash or kind) for farmers, traders, and other food system agents, lower prices for consumers or, most likely, a combination of the two as exemplified by the effects of the Green Revolution which lowered unit-costs of production of wheat and rice, increased farmers' incomes, and lowered consumer prices. A second pathway through incomes, that will change access to food, relates to changes in labor demand, wages and access to productive resources, e.g., land and water, through labor-using technology, investments in rural infrastructure, changes in land tenure and water policies, and other fiscal and monetary policies. Thirdly, changes in the food system may change the gender-specific income control as well as the composition of household incomes (cash or production for own consumption), and the cash flow over time (Figure 3). Those changes will influence household food acquisition behavior and the extent to which access is converted to acquisition. It is also likely to influence the allocation of food among household members. Increasing income and budget control by women is likely to increase the portion of household incomes dedicated to food, particularly as it relates to child feeding. Reducing poverty is important but insufficient to eliminate deficiencies and may contribute to obesity (Ecker, Breisinger, and Pauw 2012; Rajkumar, Gaukler, and Tilahun 2012).

While food supply chains are becoming longer in most African countries, locavore campaigns to prioritize the consumption of locally produced food are attempting to shorten supply chains in higher-income countries by bringing farmers and consumers together at farmers markets and reducing or eliminating the input from other market agents. It is interesting to note that both the lengthening of the supply chain driven by supermarkets and better storage and transportation facilities in developing countries and the shortening in higher-income countries may reduce nutrient losses and food safety risks Expanding urban agriculture and kitchen gardens may also shorten the food supply chain.

The demand for organically produced food is increasing rapidly in higher-income countries. Organic production methods may have positive health effects due to reductions in the use of pesticides, antibiotic, and other inorganic chemical agents and smallholder farmers may gain from a price premium. In a recent review of available evidence Smith-Spangler et al. (2012, 348) concluded that "Consumption of organic food may reduce exposure to pesticide residues and antibiotic-resistant bacteria." The same review concluded that "the published literature lacks strong evidence that organic foods are significantly more nutritious than conventional food" (p. 348). The findings have been hotly contested in the news media, e.g., Bittman (2012). An earlier systematic review of the evidence concluded that "evidence is lacking for nutrition-related health effects that result from the consumption of organically produced foodstuffs" (Dangour et al. 2010, 203), while Worthington (2001) found that organic crops contained significantly more vitamin C, iron, magnesium, and phosphorus and less nitrates than conventional crops and she concluded that "there appear to be genuine differences in the nutrient content of organic and conventional crops" (p. 161).

As developing countries liberalize their food and agricultural markets and open up for food import, processed energy-dense food products become more readily available (Hawkes 2006; Young 2012). Both energy intake and diet diversity are likely to increase and the higher content of refined sugar, sweeteners, fats, oils, and salt and the lower content of fiber and nutrients cause obesity, increasing health risks and diet deterioration. Diet diversity is critically important for nutrition but diet diversity resulting from a shift towards more processed energy-dense foods is not what improved nutrition calls for.

Changes in food and non-food prices will influence a household's purchasing power and its access to food. Changes in relative prices among foods are important. Unit-cost reducing technological change in food production, processing and marketing as well as commodity-specific taxes and subsidies and trade restrictions are examples of policy interventions that may change relative prices. Before such commodity-specific policies are proposed, it is important to clearly specify the nutrition problem to be solved: is it dietary energy deficiencies, micronutrient deficiencies, or obesity-related chronic diseases? Can changing relative prices reduce the importance of one problem without contributing to another?

Most developing countries experience all three of these problems. This makes the choice of price-related policies difficult. For example, taxes on meat, vegetable oil, sugar, and sweeteners may reduce the risks of chronic disease among low- and high-income people while increasing the deficiency of iron, essential fatty acids, and dietary energy in low-income population groups. If these foods are highly preferred by low-income households, such taxes may also reduce purchasing power and the consumption of other foods which are beneficial for nutrition such as fruits and vegetables. Subsidies on fruits and vegetables may release purchasing power that could be used to acquire foods of lesser or negative nutrient value such as drinks high in sweeteners. Increasing productivity and lower unit-costs of production and marketing as well as price subsidies for foods such as fruits, vegetables, and animal source foods may reduce micronutrient deficiencies.

Food price fluctuations may contribute to transitory food insecurity and malnutrition. Policies to strengthen timely price information and projections might reduce such negative nutrition effects for both farmers and consumers. Incentives and regulations in the supply chain to facilitate sound competition and avoid hoarding in the food supply chain may be needed along with social safety nets to protect low-income people's nutritional status.

To the extent that they were transmitted to poor consumers, increases in international food prices during 2007–08, 2010–11, and the first half of 2012 reduced purchasing power and access to food by low-income net food buyers. The impact on diets was two-fold: a shift from more expensive calories to less expensive ones and a net reduction in the intake of dietary energy and nutrients (Iannotti and Robles 2011; Robles 2010; von Grebmer et al. 2011). Although the empirical evidence is scarce, it is likely that the former reduced diet diversity and increased micronutrient deficiencies. The latter would be harmful to those consuming too little and helpful for those at risk of overweight or obesity. Attempts by many governments to control food prices by decree generally failed unless they were accompanied by interventions in supply and/or demand such as trade policies or rationing. Export bans, such as Indian and Vietnamese bans on rice export in 2007–08 were effective in reducing or avoiding the transmission of international food prices to national markets in traditional export countries, while placing upward pressures on prices in the international market to the detriment of net-importing countries such as the Philippines (Pinstrup-Andersen, forthcoming). Social safety nets, including cash or food transfers and targeted consumer food subsidies, were implemented by several developing countries (Bryan, forthcoming). However, even though a large share of the malnourished were net-buying rural poor, most of these programs were targeted to the urban population, including the non-poor, who threatened government legitimacy (Pinstrup-Andersen, forthcoming). Investments in public goods such as rural infrastructure, market information, and certain kinds of research and technology dissemination could help smallholders to become net sellers while facilitating private sector investments and reduced price and production fluctuations at the local levels.

It is unlikely that real food prices will continue to increase. There was a need for a food price adjustment in the beginning of this century. This has now taken place and the long-run real food price trend is likely to be slightly falling. It is very likely that the high degree of food price volatility will continue and possibly increase in the future due to continued extreme weather events caused by climate change and the reactions by governments and speculators to amplify price fluctuations as experienced during 2007–08, 2010–11, and the first half of 2012.

Refinement of WTO rules against unjustified and abrupt changes in food exports resulting in large changes in international food prices and consideration of new rules might reduce the temptation faced by exporting countries to alter trade policies at the expense of the rest of the world. A new set of rules of behavior for speculators in futures markets could also reduce the severity of future price volatility. Public and privately funded research to develop new food crop varieties tolerant to drought, floods, strong winds, and new biotic risks associated with climate change would be useful to reduce production fluctuations.

Economic growth, urbanization, and globalization contribute to the diet transition, enlarges the supply chain, and place new demands on the food system likely to result in changes in relative food prices. Fruits, vegetables, and animal source foods are likely to be more expensive relative to staples such as maize and cassava although staple prices will be supported by the demand for animal feed and raw material for biofuel. If these relative price changes are driven by dietary changes among the non-poor, the poor and malnourished will respond by consuming more staples and less fruits, vegetables, and foods of animal origin. The result may be further increases in micronutrient deficiencies, overweight, and obesity, resulting from excessive energy intake and reductions in diet diversity. Economic growth and urbanization move consumer demand towards higher quality food, an increasing concern for food safety, a more diverse diet shifting from grains to animal source foods and more convenience foods. This demand change is paralleled by the expansion of supermarkets in most developing countries (Reardon et al. 2003; Reardon, Henson, and Berdegue 2007). The share of the consumer outlay that is captured by the farmer decreases and the post-harvest portion of the food value chain, e.g., processing, fortification, and storage, increases. The supply chain becomes longer and the effect of agricultural policies, such as price policies, on consumers and their nutrition becomes less pronounced, while policies focused on food processing gain importance (Hawkes, Turner, and Wage 2012b). Promotion of value chains in which health and nutrition goals play a major role offers new opportunities for strengthening the health and nutrition effects of the food system (Gomez and Ricketts 2012). A potential conflict between food safety standards and food security may develop when the former results in higher food prices (Caswell and Friis Bach 2007).

Knowledge

Improved knowledge regarding nutrition and its relations to the food system is needed for consumers, farmers, traders, and policymakers. Nutrition education and dissemination of information through labeling and social marketing for consumers has been commonly used to improve nutrition but with limited success. As might be expected, free-standing nutrition education programs will only be successful where lack of knowledge is the most limiting factor for good nutrition. Labeling, in turn, will only be useful to consumers if they have the necessary knowledge to interpret the label. Labeling can communicate misinformation by making unsubstantiated claims or claims that are clearly incorrect. There may, of course, be reasons to label food other than health risk. Labeling may be seen as a means to differentiate foods, a goal similar to private branding. However, it is important that neither private branding nor labeling make unsubstantiated health claims. Promotion of unhealthy processed foods leading to obesity, chronic diseases, and micronutrient deficiencies is unfortunately common. While the suppliers of such food claim that they are merely meeting consumer demand, such demand may be created by the suppliers. In view of the severe public health and economic implications of the rapidly increasing prevalence of obesity, diabetes and other chronic diseases, and the widespread micronutrient deficiencies, governments may wish to intervene through regulation, incentives, and knowledge campaigns.

Educational efforts with all the right messages may be of no value if the new knowledge cannot be implemented because of time or income constraints. Similarly, increased incomes may be of little or no nutrition value in the absence of the relevant knowledge. Therefore, nutrition education should be combined with other efforts to remove constraints to good nutrition. Improved knowledge regarding food storage, processing, and transportation may reduce losses, including deteriorations of the nutrition value. In some cases, the achievements of nutrition goals may imply trade-offs with other goals but multiple-wins are common and often overlooked. Examples include investments in rural infrastructure, agricultural research, food processing technology, nutrition education, and market information, which may increase food production, reduce unit-costs of production and marketing, reduce consumer prices, increase farmer incomes, and improve nutrition. Having nutritional improvements as one of the goals of interventions in the food system is preferable to the relegation of nutrition improvements to narrowly-focused food system interventions with the sole objective of nutrition improvement. Nutrition should be mainstreamed in food system interventions instead of relegated to a set of small projects. As discussed later, this poses serious challenges for the evaluation of impact.

Time Allocation

Opportunities in the food system for improving—or harming—the nutritional status of pregnant and lactating women and children during the first two years of life (the first 1,000 days following conception) are related to how the food system affects women's time allocation. Policies often seek to empower women and improve their wellbeing as well as that of children by attempting to generate gender-specific employment. However, some employment makes breastfeeding, which is critically important during the first six months of life and beyond, very difficult either because employment takes the lactating mother away from the baby for long periods or because the employment activities are otherwise incompatible with breastfeeding. Furthermore, employment creation by women may harm nutrition by reducing their time available for other important nutrition-related activities such as care, cooking, fetching water and firewood, and agricultural work. Thus, changes in the food system should consider the net effect of changes in women's time before introducing new demands for women's work. Ideally, ex ante estimates would be based on total household time and efforts should be made to facilitate substitution among adults, e.g., between women and men. Introduction of labor-saving and productivity-enhancing technologies for the work traditionally done by women, such as herbicides to replace weeding, improved equipment for food processing, better access to water and fuel, and rural infrastructure to improve food marketing, and the time needed to bring food to the market as well as child care facilities appropriate for the particular situation, are examples of actions that could be considered and supported by governments.

An Additional Behavioral Issue

A number of behavioral issues related to each of the steps in Figure 3 were discussed above. Many others are relevant to the topic of this article. One of these is the extent to which decisions are made on the basis of rationality. The five factors: food availability, prices, incomes, time availability, and knowledge may be perceived as providing the boundaries within which households make their food and health- related decisions. In an ideal world, nutrition needs would be represented in household and individual wants which in turn would be represented in demand. In the absence of the above constraints, the market would be expected to fulfill these demands. In the real world, the constraints exist and the demand is likely to be influenced by a list of factors some of which are mentioned above. Assuming rationality, and given their goals, preferences and constraints, the consumer would seek to meet wants (but not necessarily needs) subject to the cost of achieving them. In addition to removing or reducing the impact of the constraints, government intervention might attempt to change consumer behavior to reduce the gap between perceived and real needs, as well as the gap between needs and wants and the gap between wants and demand.

However, recent behavioral research suggests that "the potential for information-based interventions is fundamentally limited, given that it is based on a view of human behavior that is at odds with psychological and neuroscientific evidence that much human behavior is not actually driven by deliberations upon the consequences of action, but is automatic, cued by stimuli in the environment" (Marteau, Hollands, and Fletcher 2012). These findings need not conflict with the assumption that consumers make decisions on the basis of utilitarianism. Overeating leading to obesity by consumers with a high internal discount rate for time and a low perceived risk of getting diabetes or other chronic diseases from obesity may be rational from a utilitarian perspective, particularly if society pays for healthcare. However, if consumption decisions are made primarily by cues in the environment, the way out for policy advisors may be to focus on re-arranging the environment to produce the cues needed to achieve health and nutrition goals. A large number of experiments by Wansink (2006) would support that conclusion. If these new findings are interpreted to mean that utilitarianism plays an important role in some but not all decisions, the question becomes how to design activities such as nutrition education for maximum effect. That, of course, is not a new question.

A key policy question related to behavior is to what extent food systems (supply factors) influence household and individual food consumption (demand factors) because the answer to that question will help design and implement effective policies. At the one extreme it can be argued that the supply chain responds to what the consumers demand. Thus, policies to change diets to improve nutrition should be focused on demand behavior. At the other extreme, some argue that supply decisions, particularly advertising and promotion by the food system and the design of processed food, influence consumer behavior and determine what is being consumed. If this is true, policies should try to change supply behavior. The answer is context-specific and more research is needed to guide policy in particular contexts.

Policy Implementation

Nutrition presents very interesting institutional challenges because, contrary to agriculture and health, it is not a sector and it does not have a ministerial home in governments. It is, in the words of Mwadime (2012, 153) "a cross-cutting development problem that needs to be integrated into the activities and policies of the agriculture, health, education, and sanitation and water sectors (among others), and featured in the priorities of broader agencies such as ministries of finance and gender." This is extremely difficult (Garrett and Natalicchio 2011; Hill, Gonzalez, and Pelletier 2011), but not impossible. Examples of successful integration of nutrition into several existing ministries and programs include Brazil's Zero Hunger program, Bolivia's Zero Malnutrition program, the nutrition program in Thailand and the REACH program in Lao PDR and Mauritania (Kepple, Maluf, and Burlandy 2012; Hoey and Pelletier 2011; Pearson and Ljungqvist 2011). Recent initiatives by international organizations, including the World Bank, FAO, CAADP (Comprehensive Africa Agriculture Development), and UNICEF (United Nations Children's Fund), to mainstream nutrition in national and international strategies are expected to further promote successful institutional developments although the jury is still out.

Evidence Gaps and Research Needs

The impact of food system policies on nutrition and health has not been rigorously evaluated and compiled in the same manner as direct health and nutrition interventions. The main reason was given by Bhutta et al. (2008) in a *Lancet* article in which they concluded that "Interventions to diversify diets by enhancement of agriculture and small-animal production... are potentially promising and culturally relevant, but in general, have only been implemented at a small scale, and have not been adequately assessed. In view of the weak evidence for the effects of these interventions on human nutrition, we did not attempt to estimate their effects." The problem is that evaluation methods based on randomized controlled trials (RCTs)—the gold standard and usually the only methods perceived to provide reliable results in the health sector—are generally impossible to apply to the food system except for small, usually insignificant projects for two reasons. First, the pathways are long and influenced by a large number of variables including uncontrollable behavior by system agents and second, large policy interventions in food systems do not lend themselves to a control group. Yet, the big and promising opportunities for nutrition improvements are undoubtedly found in such policies and not in home gardens and other minor projects where RCTs can be used (Pinstrup-Andersen 2013a; 2013b). A recent report that reviewed the available literature and summarized outcomes of agricultural policies on nutrition found very little impact on child nutritional status and concluded that the lack of impact might be due to weaknesses in the evaluations rather than inherent weaknesses of the interventions themselves (Masset et al. 2011).

In a recent *Lancet* article, Ruel and Alderman (2013) concluded that the evidence for nutrition improvements resulting from interventions in food systems is inconclusive. Yet, impact path evaluations show that such interventions can have very significant positive effects on the elements of the pathways discussed above and that changes in these elements can have significant positive effects on under-nutrition.

While more research is urgently needed, Ruel and Alderman (2013) suggest a set of research priorities, characterizing current evidence as inconclusive invalidates existing evidence from impact path assessments and sends what I believe to be a wrong message to policymakers not to pursue nutrition-sensitive policies for the food system.

Lack of knowledge about how interventions in the food system affect obesity presents a serious evidence gap. Very few evaluations and no literature review have been done on this subject. An exception is a study of the obesity impact of the U.S. agricultural policies (Alston, Rickard, and Okrent 2010). The study's conclusion that the policies, when taken together, has not contributed to obesity, has been challenged by the Physicians Committee for Responsible Medicine which, under the headlines of "Agriculture and Health Policies in Conflict, How Food Subsidies Tax Our Health", concluded that U.S. agricultural subsidies have contributed very significantly to obesity (PCRM 2012). The main reason for the different findings may be that Alston, Rickard, and Okrent (2010) assesses the whole U.S. agricultural policy while PCRM focuses on parts.

Concluding Comments

Malnutrition causes large economic losses and widespread human suffering. Measures to correct what may be considered a market failure are plentiful. This paper addresses one set of such measures—nutrition-sensitive policies for the food system—which has been all but ignored by policymakers (Appendix). Failure to explicitly consider nutrition goals in the design and implementation of food system policies has resulted in large benefits foregone. While trade-offs between achieving nutrition goals and other food system goals must be confronted, complementarities and multiple wins are possible. The main reasons why the market has been unable to effectively address the nutrition goals is that nutrition needs are frequently not reflected in economic demand. This discrepancy is caused by a large number of factors including poverty, household behavior, time constraints, and other factors shown in Figure 3. The key nutrition-related role of policy interventions in the food system is to remove the discrepancy. While a combination of food system policies and direct nutrition interventions should be pursued, the design and implementation of the package of interventions is context-specific. This paper has attempted to suggest a foundation for such efforts, including pathways expected to be of general relevance.

While waiting for more research to strengthen the evidence base, a number of policy interventions including those mentioned in this article, may be considered. It is critically important that the relevant pathways and intervention points are identified and that the environment within which the challenge exists is fully understood. A political economy approach, in which the policy process and the relevant stakeholder groups, their objectives and relative power are understood, is most likely to succeed. Merely assuming that improved nutrition overrides all other food system goals, even if the head of state or some other high-level decision-maker declares that it is so, will lead to disappointing results. Instead, efforts should be made to identify multiple-win strategies in which nutrition goals can be achieved along with other goals of importance to the constellation of stakeholder groups.

Policies that: (1) expand incomes of households with malnourished members; (2) reduce unit cost in food production with emphasis on food crops and livestock that contribute to a more diverse diet with higher content of micronutrients; (3) include women explicitly in policy design and implementation; (4) does not add to women's time demand without simultaneously reducing their time demand in other activities; and (5) provide incentives and introduce regulations in the value chain and households to reduce the consumption of energy-dense, nutrient-poor processed foods, are likely to be relevant in most situations.

References

Alston, J.M., B.J. Rickard, and A.M. Okrent. 2010. "Farm Policy and Obesity in the United States." *Choices* 25 (3). http://farmdoc.illinois.edu/policy/choices/20103/201031.pdf

Arimond, M., C. Hawkes, M.T. Ruel, Z. Sifri, P.R. Berti, J.L. Leroy, J.W. Low, L.R. Brown, and E.A. Frongillo. 2011. "Agricultural Interventions and Nutrition: Lessons From the Past and New Eevidence." *In Combating Micronutrient Deficiencies: Food-based Approaches*, edited by B. Thompson, and L. Amoroso, 41-75. Rome: Food and Agriculture Organization of the United Nations and CAB International.

Bhutta, Z.A., T. Ahmed, R.E. Black, S. Cousens, K. Dewey, E. Giugliani, B.A. Haider, B. Kirkwood, S.S. Morris, H.P.S. Sachdev, and M. Shekar. 2008. "Maternal and Child Undernutrition 3: What Works? Interventions for Maternal and Child Undernutrition and Survival." *The Lancet* 371 (9610): 417-40.

Bittman, M. 2012. "That Flawed Stanford Study." Opinionator, *The New York Times*, October 2. http://opinionator.blogs.nytimes.com/2012/10/02/that-flawed-stanford-study/.

Bouis, H.E., C. Hotz, B. McClafferty, J.V. Meenaskshi, and W.H. Pfeiffer. 2011. "Biofortification: A New Tool to Reduce Micronutrient Malnutrition." *Food and Nutrition Bulletin* 32 (1) (Supplement): S31-S40.

Bryan, S. Forthcoming. "A Cacophony of Policy Responses: Evidence from 14 Countries During the 2007/08 Food Price Crisis." In *Food Price Policy in an Era of Market Instability: A Political Economy Analysis*, edited by P. Pinstrup-Andersen. London: Oxford University Press.

Caswell, J.A., and C. Friis Bach. 2007. "Food Safety Standards in Rich and Poor Countries." In *Ethics, Hunger and Gglobalization—In Search of Appropriate Policies*, edited by P. Pinstrup-Andersen, and P. Sandøe, 281-304. Dordrecht: Springer.

Cotula, L., S. Vermeulen, R. Leonard, and J. Keeley. 2009. *Land Grab or Development Opportunity: Agricultural Investment and International Land Deals in Africa*. London/Rome: IIED/FAO/IFAD.

Dangour, A.D., K. Lock, A. Hayter, A. Aikenhead, E. Allen, and R. Uauy. 2010. "Nutrition-Related Health Effects of Organic Foods: A Systematic Review." *American Journal of Clinical Nutrition* 92: 203-10.

Deininger, K., and D. Byerlee. 2011. *Rising Global Interest in Farmland: Can it Yield Sustainable and Equitable Benefits?* Washington, DC: The World Bank.

Ecker, O., C. Breisinger, and K. Pauw. 2012. "Growth is Good, but is not Enough to Improve Nutrition." Chapter 6. In *Reshaping Agriculture for Nutrition and Health*, edited by S. Fan, and R. Pandya-Lorch, 47-54. Washington, DC: International Food Policy Research Institute.

Garrett, J., and M. Natalicchio. 2011. *Working Multisectorally in Nutrition: Principles, Practices, and Case Studies*. Washington, DC: International Food Policy Research Institute.

German, L., G. Schoneveld, and E. Mwangi. 2011. "Processes of Large-scale Land Acquisition by Investors: Case Studies for Sub-Saharan Africa." Paper presented at the International Conference on Global Land Grabbing, April 6–8, 2011, Institute of Development Studies, University of Sussex.

Gillespie, S., L. Haddad, V. Mannar, P. Menon, and N. Nisbett. 2013. "The Politics of Reducing Malnutrition: Building Commitment and Accelerating Impact." *The Lancet on-line*. Accessed June 6, 2013. http://dx.doi.org/10.1016/s0140-6736(13)6084-9..

Gillespie, S., and S. Kadiyala. 2012. "Exploring the Agriculture-Nutrition Disconnect in India." Chapter 20. In *Reshaping Agriculture for Nutrition and Health*, edited by S. Fan and R. Pandya-Lorch, 173-82. Washington, DC: International Food Policy Research Institute.

Gomez, M.I., and K. Ricketts. 2012. "Food Value Chains and Policies Influencing Nutritional Outcomes." Background paper for the State of Food and Agriculture 2013: Food Systems for Better Nutrition. Food and Agriculture Organization of the United Nations, Rome.

Gustavsson, J., C. Cederberg, U. Sonesson, R. van Otterdijk, and A. Meybeck. 2011. *Global Food Losses and Food Waste*. Study conducted for the International Congress "Save Food!" at Interpack2011, Düsseldorf, Germany. Rome: Food and Agriculture Organization of the United Nations.

Hawkes, C. 2006. *Uneven Dietary Development: Linking the Policies and Processes of Globalization with the Nutrition Transition, Obesity and Diet-related Chronic Diseases. Globalization and Health*. Washington, DC: International Food Policy Research Institute.

Hawkes, C. 2007. "Promoting Healthy Diets and Tackling Obesity and Diet-related Chronic Diseases: What are the Agricultural Policy Levers?" *Food and Nutrition Bulletin* 28 (Suppl. 2): S312-S322.

Hawkes, C., S. Friel, T. Lobstein, and T. Lang. 2012a. "Linking Agricultural Policies with Obesity and Noncommunicable Diseases: A New Perspective for a Globalizing World." *Food Policy* 37 (3): 343-53.

Hawkes, C., and C. Ruel. 2006. "Agriculture and Nutrition Linkages: Old Lessons and New Paradigms." In *Understanding the Links between Agriculture and Health*, edited by C. Hawkes, and M.T. Ruel, 2020 Focus 13, Brief 4. Washington, DC: International Food Policy Research Institute.

Hawkes, C., R. Turner, and J. Wage. 2012b. "Current and Planned Research on Agriculture for Improved Nutrition: A Mapping and a Gap Analysis." A Report for DFID, Leverhulme Centre for Integrative Research on Agriculture and Health (LCIRAH) and Centre for Sustainable International Development, University of Aberdeen.

Herforth, A. 2012. *Synthesis of Guiding Principles on Agriculture Programming for Nutrition*. FAO. http://www.securenutritionplatform.org/pages/displayresources.aspx?RID=32

Herforth, A., A. Jones, and P. Pinstrup-Andersen, P. 2012. "Prioritizing Nutrition in Agriculture and Rural Development: Guiding Principles for Operational Investments." HNP Discussion Paper Series. Washington, DC: The World Bank.

Hill, R., W. Gonzalez, and D.L. Pelletier. 2011. "The Formulation of Consensus on Nutrition Policy: Policy Actors' Perspectives on Good Process." *Food and Nutrition Bulletin* 32 (2): S92-S104.

Hoddinott, J. 2012. "Agriculture, Health, and Nutrition: Toward Conceptualizing the Linkages," Chapter 2. In *Reshaping Agriculture for Nutrition and Health*, edited by. S. Fan, and R. Pandya-Lorch, 13-20. Washington, DC: International Food Policy Research Institute.

Hoey, L., and D.L. Pelletier. 2011. "Bolivia's Multisectoral Zero Malnutrition Program: Insights on Commitment, Collaboration, and Capacities." *Food and Nutrition Bulletin* 32 (2): S70-S81.

Iannotti, L., and M. Robles. 2011. "Negative Impact on Calorie Intake Associated with the 2006–08 Food Price Crisis in Latin America." *Food and Nutrition Bulletin* 32 (2): 112-23.

Jones, A. 2011. "Overcoming Barriers to Improving Infant and Young Child Feeding Practices in the Bolivian Andes: The Role of Agriculture and Rural Livelihoods." PhD diss., Cornell University.

Kennedy, E., H. Bouis, and J. von Braun. 1992. "Health and Nutrition Effects of Cash-crop Production in Developing Countries: A Comparative Analysis." *Social Science and Medicine* 35: 689-97.

Kepple, A.W., R.S. Maluf, and L. Burlandy. 2012. Case Study (9-10)—"Implementing A Decentralized National Food and Nutrition Security System in Brazil." In *Food Policy for Developing Countries: Case Studies*, edited by P. Pinstrup-Andersen. cip.cornell.edu/gfs.

Low, J.W., M. Arimond, N. Osman, B. Cunguara, F. Zano, and D. Tschirley. 2007. "A Food-based Approach Introducing Orange-fleshed Sweet Potatoes Increased Vitamin A Intake and Serum Retinol Concentrations in Young Children in Rural Mozambique." *Journal of Nutrition* 137 (5): 1320-27.

Marteau, T.M., G.J. Hollands, and P.C. Fletcher. 2012. "Changing Human Behavior to Prevent Disease: The Importance of Targeting Automatic Processes" *Science* 337: 1492-95.

Masset, E., L. Haddad, A. Cornelius, and J. Isaza-Castro. 2011. *A Systematic Review of Agricultural Interventions that Aim to Improve Nutritional Status of Children*. London: EPPI-Centre, Social Science Research Unit, Institute of Education, University of London.

Mwadime, R.K.N. 2012. "Accelerating National Policymaking across Sectors to Enhance Nutrition.". In *Reshaping Agriculture for Nutrition and Health*, edited by S. Fan, and R. Pandya-Lorch, 153-62. Washington, DC: International Food Policy Research Institute.

National Bureau of Statistics of China. *China Statistical Yearbook 1987*. Beijing, China: National Bureau of Statistics of China.

National Bureau of Statistics of China. *China Statistical Yearbook 2010*. Beijing, China: National Bureau of Statistics of China.

Nugent, R. 2011. *Bringing Agriculture to the Table: How Agriculture and Food can Play a Role in Preventing Chronic Disease*. Chicago: Chicago Council on Global Affairs.

Oxfam. 2011. "Land and Power: The Growing Scandal Surrounding the New Wave of Investments in Land." Oxfam Briefing Paper 151. http://www.oxfam.org/sites/www.oxfam.org/files/bp151-land-power-rights-acquisitions-220911-en.pdf.

PCRM (Physicians Committee for Responsible Medicine). 2012. *Agriculture and Health Policies in Conflict: How Food Subsidies Tax our Health: Agriculture Policies Versus Health Policies*. http://www.pcrm.org/health/reports/agriculture-and-health-policies-ag-versus-health.

Pearson, B.L., and B. Ljungqvist. 2011. "REACH: An Effective Catalyst for Scaling up Priority Nutrition Interventions at the Country Level." *Food and Nutrition Bulletin* 32 (2): S115-S127.

Pinstrup-Andersen, P. 1981. "Nutritional Consequences of Agricultural Projects: Conceptual Relationships and Assessment Approaches." World Bank Staff Working Paper 456. Washington, DC: The World Bank.

Pinstrup-Andersen, P. 2012a. *Food Systems and Human Health and Nutrition: An Economic Policy Perspective with a Focus on Africa*. Center on Food Security and the Environment, Stanford Symposium Series on Global Food Policy and Food Security in the 21st Century, October 11, 2012, University of Stanford, California. http://iis-db.stanford.edu/pubs/23811/Pinstrup-Andersen_final.pdf

Pinstrup_Andersen, P. 2012b. *Guiding Food System Policies for Better Nutrition*. Background Paper for SOFA 2013. http://dyson.cornell.edu/faculty_sites/pinstrup/pdfs/SOFA.pdf

Pinstrup-Andersen, P. 2013a. "Comment: Nutrition-sensitive Food Systems: From Rhetoric to Action." *The Lancet On-line* (382) 9890: 375-76. Accessed June 6, 2013. http://www.thelancet.com/journals/lancet/article/PIIS0140-6736%2813%2961053-3/fulltext#article_upsell

Pinstrup-Andersen, P. 2013b. "Contemporary Food Policy Challenges and Opportunities." *Australian Journal of Agricultural and Resource Economics*. Wiley On-line. http://onlinelibrary.wiley.com/doi/10.1111/1467-8489.12019/full

Pinstrup-Andersen, P., ed. Forthcoming. *Food Price Policy in an Era of Market Instability: A Political Economy Analysis*. London: Oxford University Press.

Pinstrup-Andersen, P., N. Londono, and E. Hoover. 1976. "The Impact of Increasing Food Supply on Human Nutrition: Implications for Commodity Priorities in Agricultural Research and Policy." *American Journal of Agricultural Economics* 58: 131-42.

Pinstrup-Andersen, P., and D.D. Watson, II. 2011. *Food Policy for Developing Countries: The Role of Government in Global, National, and Local Food Systems*. Ithaca, NY: Cornell University Press.

Rajkumar, A.S., C. Gaukler, and J. Tilahun. 2012. *Combating Malnutrition in Ethiopia: An Evidence-based Approach for Sustained Results*. Africa Human Development Series. Washington, DC: The World Bank.

Rausser, G.C., and H. de Gorter. Forthcoming. "US Policy Contributions to Agricultural Commodity Price Fluctuations, 2006–2012." In *Food Price Policy in an Era of Market Instability: A Political Economy Analysis*, edited by P. Pinstrup-Andersen. London: Oxford University Press.

Reardon, T., S. Henson, and J. Berdegue. 2007. "Proactive Fast-tracking Diffusion of Supermarkets in Developing Countries: Implications for Market Institutions and Trade." *Journal of Economic Geography* 7 (4): 399-431.

Reardon, T., P. Timmer, C. Barrett, and J. Berdegue. 2003. "The Rise of Supermarkets in Africa, Asia, and Latin America." *American Journal of Agricultural Economics* 85 (5): 1140-1146.

Robertson, B., and P. Pinstrup-Andersen. 2010. "Global Land Acquisition: Neo-colonialism or Development Opportunity?" *Food Security* 2: 271-83.

Robles, M. 2010. "Welfare Impact of Changing Food Prices: The Case of Bangladesh, Pakistan, and Vietnam." Study prepared for the project ADB RETA 13th, Policies for Ensuring Food Security in South and Southeast Asia (November). Washington, DC: International Food Policy Research Institute.

Ruel, M.T., and H. Alderman, and the Maternal and Child Nutrition Study Group. 2013. "Nutrition-Sensitive Interventions and Programs: How Can They Help Accelerate Progress in Improving Maternal and Child Nutrition." *The Lancet On-line*. Accessed June 6, 2013..http://dx.doi.org/10.1016/s0140-6736(13)60843-0

Smith-Spangler, C., M.L. Brandeau, G.E. Hunter, J.C. Bavinger, M. Pearson, P.J. Eschbach, V. Sundaram, H. Liu, P. Schirmer, C. Stave, I. Olkin, and D.M. Bravata. 2012. "Are Organic Foods Safer or Healthier than Conventional Alternatives?" *Annals of Internal Medicine* 157: 348-66.

SUN Framework for Action. 2010. online at: http://www.scalingupnutrition.org.

Wansink, B. 2006. *Mindless Eating: Why We Eat More than We Think*. New York: Bantam Dell.

von Braun, J., and E. Kennedy, eds. 1994. *Agricultural Commercialization, Economic Development, and Nutrition*. Baltimore, MD: Johns Hopkins University Press.

von Grebmer, K., M. Torero, T. Olofinbiyi, H. Fritschel, D. Wiesmann, Y. Yohannes, L. Schofield, and C. von Oppeln. 2011. 2011 *Global Hunger Index—The Challenge of Hunger: Taming Price Spikes and Excessive Food Price Volatility*. Washington, DC: International Food Policy Research Institute, Concern Worldwide, and Welthungerhilfe.

WHO. (World Health Organization). 2004. *Global Strategy on Diet, Physical Activity and Health*. http://www.who.int/dietphysicalactivity/strategy/eb11344/strategy_english_web.pdf.

World Bank. 2007. "From Agriculture to Nutrition: Pathways, Synergies and Outcomes." Report No. 40196-GLB. Washington, DC: The World Bank.

World Bank. 2010. *Investing Across Borders: Global Indicators of FDI Regulation*. Investment Climate Advisory Services World Bank Group. Washington, DC: The World Bank.

Worthington, V. 2001. "Nutritional Quality of Organic versus Conventional Fruits, Vegetables, and Grains." *The Journal of Alternative and Complementary Medicine* 7 (2): 161-73.

Young, E.M. 2012. *Food and Development*. New York: Routledge.

Appendix

Nutrition-sensitive policies for food systems

The choice of policy interventions should be context-specific. The following list of foci for policy interventions, discussed in this article, may serve as a starting point for the design of policies that are most appropriate for a particular set of circumstances.

Nutrition-sensitive policy interventions to be considered for the rural malnourished (most of whom are in stage 1 and 2) may focus on the following objectives:

1. Enhance smallholder market access
2. Enforcement of contracts and standards
3. Improving domestic output and input markets.
4. Rural infrastructure investments
5. Risk management (markets and climate)
6. Reduction in seasonal fluctuations in food supply, incomes and prices
7. Reducing food price volatility
8. Support for village-level food fortification
9. Regulation of land grabbing

The following policy foci may be relevant for both the rural and urban malnourished (stages 1–4):

10. Reducing women's time demand
11. Empowerment of women
12. Increase women's productivity and budget control
13. Commodity-specific subsidies and taxes
14. Knowledge creation and dissemination, behavioral change
15. Improved child care, access to therapeutic foods
16. Promotion of breastfeeding
17. Social safety nets
18. Improving access to clean water
19. Improving access to good sanitation and hygiene
20. Improving access to primary healthcare
21. Subsidies for essential non-food expenses such as school fees
22. Research priorities that favor productivity increases and risk reductions for a portfolio of commodities with emphasis on expanded nutrient availability
23. Regulation of food processing, advertising, promotion, and international trade

Agricultural Productivity and Child Mortality: The Impact of the Green Revolution

Mark W. Rosegrant[1], Robert E. Evenson, Siwa Msangi[2], Timothy B. Sulser[3]

"This paper is dedicated to the memory of Robert E. Evenson. Bob was a great teacher and advisor to hundreds of students at Yale and in the Philippines, many of whom have gone on to highly successful careers. Bob was a leading scholar in research related to agri¬cultural research, economic development, and education."

Many papers have examined the impact of the Green Revolution and the international agricultural research centers on agricultural productivity and the rates of return to agricultural research investment. Here we extend this analysis to look at the impact on food security and human welfare as measured by child mortality. In this paper, we conduct two counterfactual simulations for the 30-year period 1970-2000—the first holding 1970 crop genetic improvements constant and the second presuming the International Agricultural Research Center (IARC) system had not been built. Our results show that Green Revolution technologies and the IARC system significantly reduced child mortality. The counterfactual analysis demonstrates the importance of the Green Revolution in generating not only sustained improvements in crop productivity growth through the 1970s and 1980s, but also the powerful indirect effects on human welfare as measured by child mortality.

Keywords: Agricultural productivity, Green Revolution, child mortality

1. Introduction

Agricultural productivity around the world has grown considerably over the past few decades, much of which can be attributed to agricultural research. This is especially accurate for the growth achieved during the Green Revolution period when breeding and adoption of improved crop varieties, especially rice and wheat, combined with the expanded use of fertilizers, other chemical inputs, and irrigation led to dramatic yield increases for these two crops in Asia and Latin America, beginning in the late 1960s. Although growth of public funding for agricultural research in both developing countries and Organization for Economic Cooperation and Development (OECD) countries has slowed in recent years, it has been a significant source of support for many decades. This was particularly true during the 1960s, when public agricultural research funds were more available than private funds (Alston and Pardey 1996).

[1] Corresponding author: Director, Environment and Production Technology Division, International Food Policy Research Institute (IFPRI), Washington, DC.

[2] Senior Research Fellow, Environment and Production Technology Division, International Food Policy Research Institute (IFPRI), Washington, DC.

[3] Trade and Markets Division, Economic and Social Development Department, Food and Agriculture Organization of the United Nations (FAO) (formerly IFPRI).

This was particularly true during the 1960s, when public agricultural research funds were more available than private funds (Alston and Pardey 1996).

Prior to the Green Revolution, an assessment was made of the National Agricultural Research Systems in various countries in order to determine whether there was a demonstrated need for them to be supported by a system of International Agricultural Research Centers (IARCs). These IARCs were to provide the technical expertise and knowledge that would help to overcome local barriers to effective promulgation of best-agricultural-practices and productivity enhancements at the country level, and to support the struggling agricultural economies of those regions most in need of development. Even without the eventual introduction of radical improvements in crop genetic traits, a successful argument for the positive impacts of IARCs could be made in many countries.

Numerous studies have found that public agricultural research has had a positive impact on agricultural productivity and for society as a whole, and that the impact of IARCs on agricultural development has likewise been positive in many countries. For example, a comprehensive analysis of rates of return to agricultural research and development by Alston et al. (2000) considers 292 studies with a total of 1,885 estimates published since 1953. The researchers calculate an average rate of return for research of 100 percent per year, with a median rate of 48 percent and mode of 46 percent. Separately, Evenson (2003) estimates at least half of all productivity gains since 1965 in developing countries are due to crop genetic improvement, with varieties developed by IARCs accounting for about half the crop genetic improvement. Country- and crop-specific examples also abound, such as Brazil, with crop genetic improvement programs contributing about 50 percent of the historical yield gains (Avila et al. 2003), and rice productivity over the past 40 years in Asia, where the Green Revolution is widely considered an enormous success (Hossain et al. 2003). In the United States, the rate of return to agricultural research is estimated around 45–50 percent (Fuglie and Heisey 2007; Huffman and Evenson 2006).

While many studies have looked at the impacts of public research funding on agricultural productivity and the rates of return to research, few have looked closely at the plausible impacts of declines in crop research on international agricultural production and the subsequent indirect effects on human welfare. Such an examination exposes the important linkage between agricultural productivity, wider economic growth, and human welfare such as child mortality. While there are numerous factors that can lead to the betterment of these human welfare indicators—ranging from the improved provision and accessibility to primary healthcare, increased access to clean water, and higher levels of education (especially for women)—we focus on those which relate directly to the improvement of agricultural performance, which is still where the bulk of economic activity resides in developing countries, especially for many countries in Sub-Saharan Africa. In particular, we are interested in the connection between the types of productivity improvements that can be attributed to the IARCs as well as to the Green Revolution, so we can assess their respective impacts on indicators of human welfare.

A key indicator of human welfare is child mortality. The United Nations Children's Fund (2012) estimates that the number of children who die before age 5 is approximately 7 million per year, and infectious disease is the leading cause of death. Of the total, Black et al. (2013) estimates that poor nutrition causes 45 percent of deaths in children under five or 3.1 million children per year[4]. Food and Agriculture Organization estimated child mortality in 2000 as a result of hunger was 6 million per year (FAO 2002). Separately, in an undated estimate, poor nutrition is estimated to play a role in 5 million child deaths each year (World Education Service Hunger 2013).

In this paper, we use IFPRI's International Model for Policy Analysis of Agricultural Commodities and Trade (IMPACT) to construct alternative counterfactuals that can help estimate the historical impact of agricultural research on international agricultural productivity and trade, and, by consequence, on the levels of child mortality that would have otherwise occurred between 1970 and 2000. By constructing scenarios in which innovations are stagnant or absent, we are able to gauge the impact that both the Green Revolution and the widespread dissemination of knowledge generated by IARCs have had on agricultural productivity and the livelihoods that depend on it.

A critical first step is to endogenize some of the key variables that underlie the projections of agricultural production growth made by the IMPACT model, which allows us to examine the influence of a much wider range of socioeconomic determinants and feedback effects than is possible within the usual framework of strictly exogenously specified demographic growth parameters. By simulating the IMPACT model with an endogenously determined system of demographic growth parameters, and under the alternative counterfactuals, we can project an alternative path of agri cultural growth between 1970 and 2000, and compare them with the previous baseline results of IMPACT. The model results, under the counterfactuals and the past trends, are compared with each other to gauge the impact that the Green Revolution and the supporting system of IARCs has had on the world's food situation, in terms of both agricultural productivity and production, as well as attendant impacts on hunger and malnutrition.

The rest of this paper describes the IMPACT model, the nutrition and population growth feedback system, the counterfactual methodology and simulation results, and conclusions.

2. The IMPACT Model

The International Model for Policy Analysis of Agricultural Commodities and Trade (IMPACT) was developed at the International Food Policy Research Institute (IFPRI) in the early 1990s. Since the development of the model, many publications have presented results examining the future of global food supply, demand, and trade (see, for example, Rosegrant et al. 2001; Scott, Rosegrant, and Ringler 2000; Delgado et al. 1999; 2003). Although the model has been expanded several times in recent years to include additional commodities and different regional/country groupings, in this analysis we use the structure of the original IMPACT model, which is best supported by the historical data available for the period addressed in this paper (1970–2000). The primary differences between the original IMPACT and IMPACT-Counterfactual are the replacement of the 1997 base year data with 1970 base year data (3-year average centered on 1970) and the calibration of the model to represent the historical trends in yield, area, and livestock numbers growth from 1970 to 2000.

[4] An earlier estimate indicated that 56 percent of child deaths across 53 developing countries were attributable to malnutrition's potentiating effects (Pelletier et al. 1995).

The original IMPACT model covers 36 countries or country groups and 16 commodities, including all cereals, soybeans, roots and tubers, meats, and dairy products (accounting for virtually all of the world's food and feed production and consumption). The model is specified as a set of country-level demand and supply equations linked to the rest of the world through trade. Food demand, including fresh and processed food, is a function of commodity prices, per capita income, and population growth. Feed demand is a function of livestock production, feed prices, and feeding efficiency. Crop production is determined by the area and yield response functions; area is projected as a function of crop price, irrigation investment, and estimated rates of loss of land to urbanization and land degradation. Crop yield is a function of crop price, input prices, investments in irrigation, and yield growth due to technological change. Growth in productivity due to technological change is in turn estimated by its component sources including advances in management research and, in the case of food crops, plant breeding research. Other sources of growth considered in the model include private sector investments in agricultural research and development, agricultural extension and education, markets, infrastructure, and irrigation (for additional details on the methodology, see Rosegrant, Meijer, and Cline 2002).

For the original IMPACT model (and subsequent versions), population growth is exogenously specified. This is used to calculate the per capita income levels that are the determinants of food consumption across regions.

3. Estimating a System of Nutrition-Growth Feedbacks

For this analysis, in order to estimate the effects of agricultural research on human welfare, a mechanism is developed to endogenously determine the interaction between nutrition and population growth using a system of six equations. The system contains six endogenous variables: (1) Dietary Energy Sufficiency (DES), which is a measure of calories consumed per capita, (2) birth rate, (3) death rate, (4) child mortality rate, (5) malnutrition based on weight scores, and (6) malnutrition based on height scores. Ten exogenous variables are employed to cover key economic, agricultural, demographic, and health indicators. For endogenous and exogenous variables, means for 1970 and 2000 are reported in Table 1. The system is defined below with a short description of each equation, followed by an explanation of endogenizing population growth and a description of how the system is linked to IMPACT.

3.1. The Dietary Energy Sufficiency System (DES) Specification

The Dietary Energy Sufficiency System (DES) is a six equation system estimated using 3SLS techniques. All equations are estimated in the presence of "country fixed effects." Table 2 reports estimates for the system. The six equations that embody this simultaneous system of endogenized growth are given below:

DES Equation:

The DES equation is critical to the system, since DES appears as a variable in the remaining equations in the system. DES is measured as calories consumed per capi-

Table 1. Variables Utilized in the Analysis

	Means	
	1970	**2000**
I. Endogenous Variables		
Dietary Energy Sufficiency (calories consumed per capita)	2,218	2,460
Birth rate (per 1,000 population)	43.47	31.22
Death rate (per 1,000 population)	17.04	11.31
Child mortality rate (deaths per 1,000 live births)	190.1	101.1
Malnutrition (weight "*z*" scores) percent of children 0–6 malnourished	30.0	10.2
Malnutrition (height "*z*" scores) percent of children 0–6 malnourished	32.0	27.8
II. Exogenous Variables		
GDP per capita in U.S. dollars	1,024	1,458
Real export price in U.S. dollars per mt	0.92	0.52
Agricultural scientists/million hectares of cropland	0.06	0.11
Share of agriculture in value added (percent)	29.6	22.7
Green Revolution modern variety adoption (percent)	3	26
Average schooling adult males (over 25)	2.89	5.13
Average schooling adult females (over 25)	1.95	4.11
Rural population density (per square km)	2.14	2.42
Hospital beds per million population	2.15	1.78
Physicians per million population	0.26	0.70

ta. The exogenous variables that determine DES are gross domestic product (GDP) per capita, average years of schooling of adult males (over 25 years of age), agricultural scientists per million hectares of cropland, Green Revolution Modern Variety (GRMV) adoption, the "real export price" of rice, wheat, and maize in world markets, and the share of agriculture in GDP. The coefficients for GDP per capita, average years of schooling of adult males, and GRMV adoption are expected to be positive. In contrast, the coefficient on the real export price of food grains is expected to be negative because this is, in effect, an "own" price elasticity. Similarly, the coefficient on the share of agriculture in GDP is expected to be negative because of "Engel's Law" (i.e., higher shares of agriculture in GDP means that less food is consumed). Thus, the DES equation is consistent with basic economic principles and interrelationships.

Birth Rate Equation:

The birth rate equation includes three variables: the average years of schooling of adult females (over 25), hospital beds per million population, and the DES variable. Studies have shown that the schooling of adult females matters more than the schooling of adult males in contraception decisions. The coefficient on hospital beds is expected to be positive, and the coefficient on the DES variable is expected to be negative because as DES goes up, contraception increases.

Death Rate Equation:

The exogenous variables for the death rate equation are the average schooling of both adult males and females (expected to be negative), physicians per million population (expected to be negative), rural population density (expected to be positive because urban areas have more services), and the endogenous DES variable (expected to be negative). We note that the DES coefficient reduces both birth and death rates. Since the birth rate and the death rate are denominated in population units, the difference in birth and death rates allows for the population growth to be "endogenized."

Child Mortality Equation:

In the child mortality rate equation, the exogenous variables included are the average years of schooling of adult females (expected to be negative because mothers specialize in child care and care for sick children), physicians per million population (expected to be negative because more doctors can cure far more children), rural population density (expected to be negative because urban areas have better health services), and the endogenous DES variable (expected to be negative because better fed children live longer).

Malnutrition (W) Equation/Malnutrition (H) Equation:

The two malnutrition equations (the first based on weight, the second on height) include four exogenous variables: GDP per capita (not significant), schooling of adult females (expected to be negative), rural population density (expected to be negative), and the endogenous DES variable (expected to be negative). These expectations (except for GDP per capita) are borne out in the estimate.

---

[5] Note that child mortality is denominated in terms of births, not in terms of population as it is for birth rates and death rates.

DES Equation:

$$DES = 229.34 + 0.00604\left(GDP/_{cap}\right) + 5.134\,AVYSCM + 19.063\,AGSCMHA$$
$$+ 0.271\,GRMV_{adoption} - 3.398\,REALExpPrice - 0.3078\,ShAgrGDP$$

Birth Rate Equation:

$$BIRTH = 6.154 - 0.4388\,AVYSCF + 0.0137\,HospBeds/Pop - 0.000535\,DES$$

Death Rate Equation:

$$DEATH = 2.706 - 0.1194\,AVYSCFM - \frac{0.0277\,Phys}{Pop} - 0.1097\,RurPopDensity - 0.000449\,DES$$

Child Mortality Equation:

$$ChMORT = \begin{pmatrix} 0.0482 - 0.001528\,AVYSCM - \dfrac{0.00105\,Physician}{Pop} \\ -0.001515\,RurPopDensity - 0.0000117\,DES \end{pmatrix} / BIRTH$$

Malnutrition (W) Equation:

$$MalnWgt = 63.76 - \frac{0.0002\,GDP}{Per\,capita} - 1.499\,AVYSCF - 1.314\,RurPopDensity - 0.0177\,DES$$

Malnutrition (H) Equation:

$$MalnHgt = 77.83 - \frac{0.005\,GDP}{Per\,Capita} - 0.7757\,AVYSCF - 0.1677\,RurPopDensity - 0.0240\,DES$$

3.2. Endogenizing Population Growth

There are two ways to endogenize population growth within the equation system. The first is to note the birth rates and death rates are denominated per 1,000 population. Thus, the difference between birth rates and death rates is the rate of growth of population. Table 1 shows that mean birth rates declined from 43.5 in 1970 to 31.2 in 2000, and that death rates declined from 17 to 11.3. This is consistent with the demographic transition model where when both birth and death rates are high, population growth is low. Typically, death rates (particularly infant and child death rates) decline before birth rates decline. Since most if not all developing countries are in demographic transitions that are quite rapid (and driven by the DES variable), the mean data for 1970 and 2000 are consistent with this.

The second method for endogenizing population growth is to note that the child mortality variable measures child deaths before age five[5]. Given that we have data on numbers of births per year for all major developing countries, we can calculate child mortality rates directly, and use these data to directly calibrate the economically driven population response within our model. Note that the DES effects on child mortality are very strong. In almost all countries when children survive to age 5, they typically survive for many more years.

Figures 1a–c show the calibration of the DES system, when it is simulated over the historical record with the observed variable values, and the results are compared to the actual population levels in various countries. As we can see, the results for both South Asia (Figure 1a) and the largest countries in the Latin American region (Figure 1b) show very good levels of fit over the entire historical record. Even the results for Sub-Saharan Africa (Figure 1c) show excellent levels of fit, with only slight deviations for short time periods in Nigeria—the most populous country in the Sub-Saharan region, by far.

There are a number of challenges that must be overcome when trying to fit a globally estimated relationship to fit country-level historical results. The obvious one is that of trying to reconcile a global level of fit—even with very favorable "goodness-of-fit" statistics with the necessary country-level exact calibration, that is needed to track population growth accurately over time. In order to do this, we estimated additional country-specific calibrating terms that enabled us to achieve the level of fit seen in Figure 1(a–c), in addition to the coefficient terms already reported in Table 2. An additional challenge was matching the spatial definitions of the model we use, to the changing of political boundaries that occur over the historical record we are observing (e.g. the break-up of the Soviet Union and Yugoslavia).

While we do know that migration plays a role in country-level changes in population, over time, we do not include this effect specifically in the modeling framework. Doing so would require a more comprehensive framework, taking into account the general equilibrium-related effects that drive total economic growth and returns to labor that are reflected in market-level wages across countries. Adding this effect into the model is left for future development, and might draw upon the data and methodology used in models such as the International Futures model (Hughes and Hillebrand 2006).

Figure 1 (a) Simulation of DES-driven Population Growth in India and Pakistan.

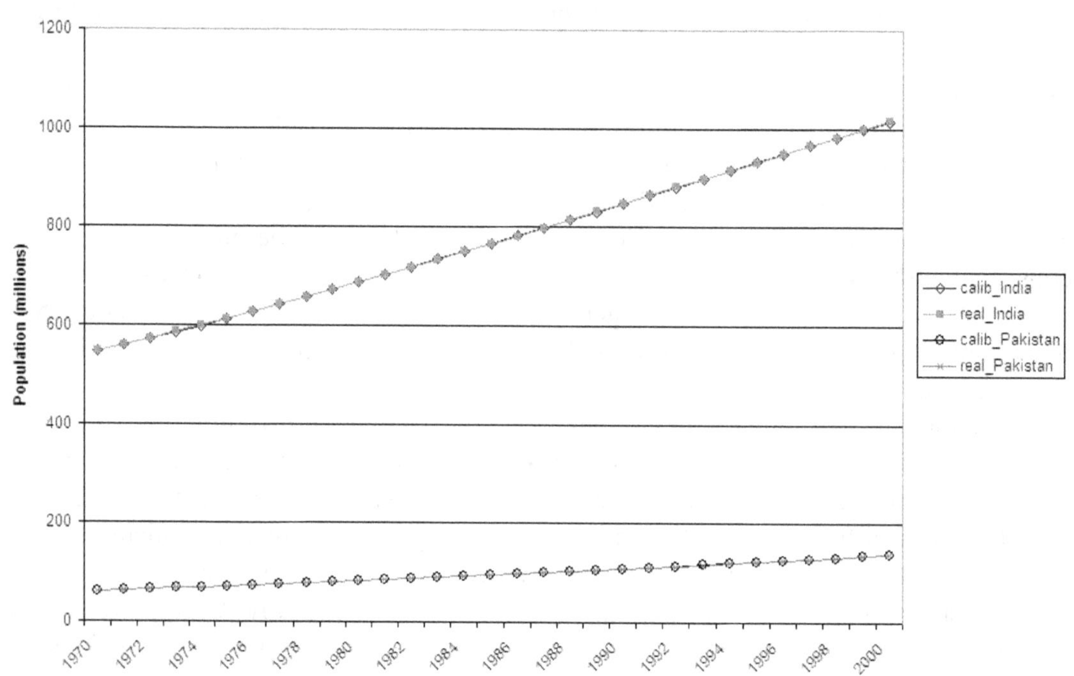

(b) Simulation of DES-driven Population Growth in Mexico and Brazil.

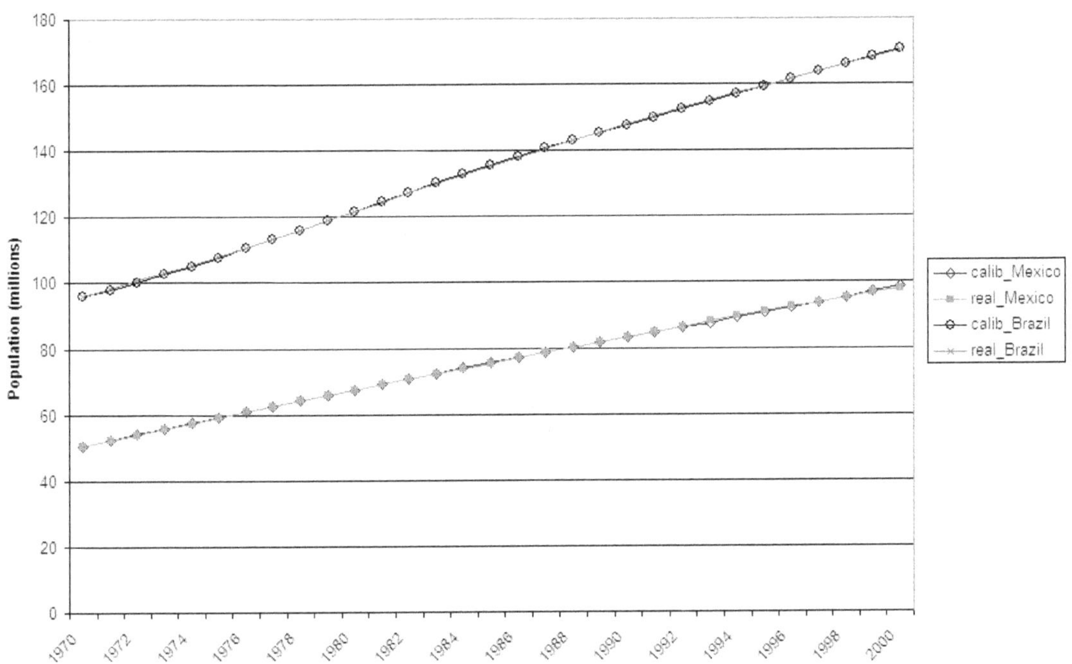

(c) Simulation of DES-driven Population Growth in Sub-Saharan Africa

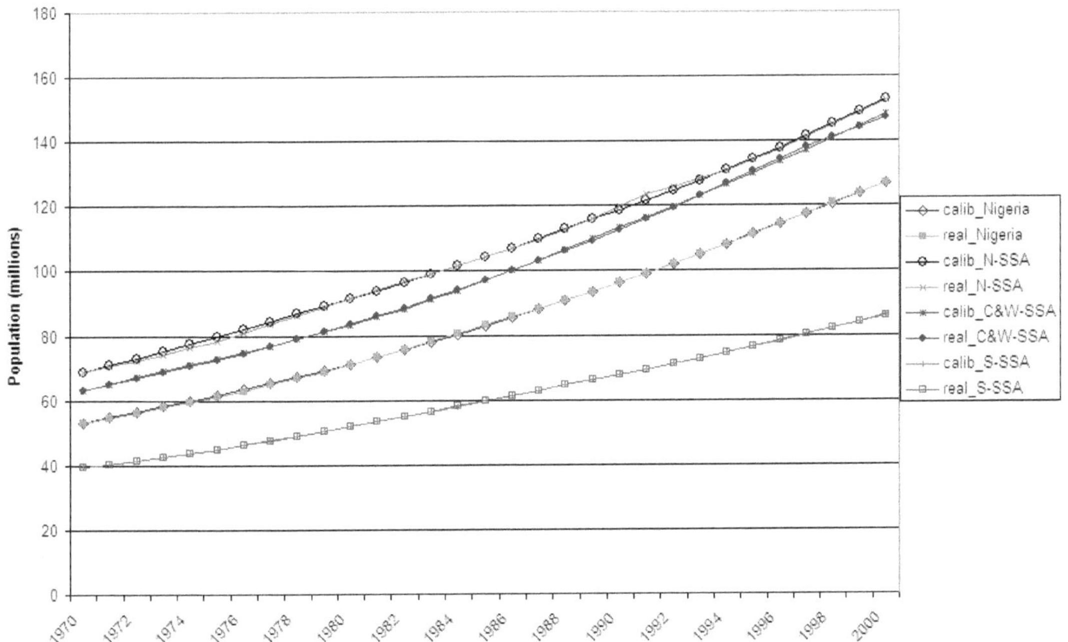

Table 2. Six Equation System: Estimated by 3SLS Techniques with Country Fixed Effects

	Dependent variables (*t* ratios in parenthesis)					
Independent variables	**DES**	**Birth rate**	**Death rate**	**Child mortality**	**Malnutrition (W)**	**Malnutrition (H)**
Constant	2293.4	25.06	27.06	0.482	63.76	77.83
	(25.92)	(7.06)	(9.07)	(14.25)	(9.56)	(9.66)
GDP/Capita	0.0604				–0.0002	0.0005
	(2.72)				(0.28)	(0.63)
AYSCM	51.34					
	(4.47)					
AGSC/MHA	190.63					
	(2.24)					
GRMV adoption	2.71					
	(3.18)					
Real export price	–33.98					
	(2.07)					
ShAgr in GDP	–3.078					
	(2.30)					
AVYSCF		–4.388		–0.01528	–1.499	–0.7757
		(19.57)		(7.49)	(4.18)	(1.80)
AVYSCF&M			–1.194			

Table 2. (Cont'd)

AVYSCF&M			–1.194			
			(6.22)			
Hosp		0.137				
beds/million pop		(0.48)				
Physicians/milli			–0.277	–0.0105		
on pop			(0.77)	(2.42)		
Rural population			–1.097	–0.01515	–1.314	–0.1677
density			(4.56)	(5.44)	(2.40)	(0.26)
DES		–0.00535	–0.00449	–0.00011	–0.0177	–0.0240
		(3.41)	(3.56)	7	(6.32)	(7.15)
				(8.67)		
R^2	0.823	0.935	0.901	0.906	0.931	0.862
Chi^2	1,830	5,648	3,499	4,011	5,507	3,106
P	0.0000	0.0000	0.0000	0.0000	0.0000	0.0000

Figure 2. Linking of DES-driven Demographics with the IMPACT model

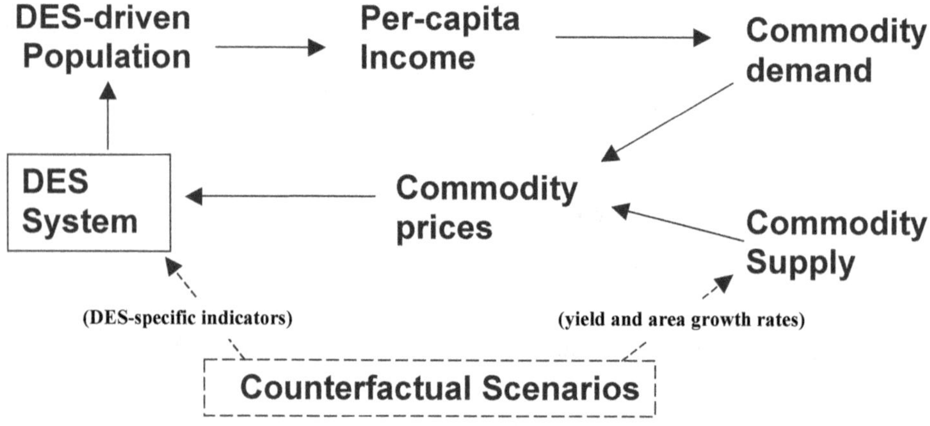

3.3. Linking the Dietary Energy Sufficiency System to IMPACT

Figure 2 shows how the DES equation system is linked with IMPACT in order to implement the counterfactual scenarios. Whereas the population growth is usually exogenously specified within IMPACT, so as to calculate the per capita income levels that are the determinants of food consumption across regions, IMPACT is linked instead directly to the output of the DES equation system for these scenarios. This very important linkage requires the population outputs to be "well-behaved," so as not to throw off the equilibrium between supply and demand in food commodity markets that is endogenously determined within the model—and the good levels of fit shown in Figures 1(a–c) assure us that this property holds.

The other key linkage shown in Figure 2 is between the scenario-specified growth rates for crop area and yield that are fed into the model on the supply side. These rates of yield improvement and crop area expansion (or contraction) are exogenously specified within IMPACT, and remain so for this scenario exercise—except that, now, they are reduced and set at levels consistent with yield improvements that would have been expected in the absence of the Green Revolution or the development of the IARC system. The nature of these scenarios with respect to productivity growth is explained in the following section.

4. Counterfactual Methodology and Simulation Results

The counterfactual experiment entailed here is to reduce the crop genetic improvement component associated with the Green Revolution. Since some countries in Sub-Saharan Africa either did not have a Green Revolution or had a modest level of GRMV adoption, the subtraction of CGI gains will have little impact on these countries. Nevertheless, the main force of the Green Revolution was to propel successful Green Revolution countries onto a sustained path of economic growth.

The analytic approach used in this paper is the same as the counterfactual methodology and yield assumptions developed in Evenson and Rosegrant (2003), which examined the economic consequences of CGI and impacts on caloric availability and the reductions in child malnourishment[6]. The counterfactual simulations allow for comparisons of equilibria where CGI growth components are removed from the base case equilibria.

Two scenarios set up to measure the impact of CGI on yield growth: (1) no Green Revolution and (2) no IARC. The first scenario reduces all crop yields to 1965 levels of genetic technology, and adjusts them going forward to reflect expected yield growth without effects of the Green Revolution. This is done by subtracting from trend yield an estimate of the contribution of CGIs to yield growth. Across all regions and crops, the average contribution of CGIs to yield growth was 0.676 in the 1960s, 0.832 in the 1980s, and 0.823 in the 1990s. For the second scenario, an estimate of the portion of yield gains attributed to varieties developed by IARCs is subtracted from trend yields. For the time period 1965–2000, the contribution was 0.36 for varietal crosses made in IARCs. The estimated contributions to yield growth used as assumptions in both scenarios (by crop) appear in Evenson (2003).

[6] Eleven crops were included in the Green Revolution part of the study: rice, wheat, maize, sorghum, pearl millet, barley, beans, groundnuts, lentils, cassava, and potatoes.

Table 3. Productivity Changes in Counterfactual Cases Relative to Actual Productivity

	No IARC			No Green Revolution		
	1970s	1980s	1990s	1970s	1980s	1990s
	Percentage points per year					
Wheat yield changes						
LA	−0.63	−0.75	−0.37	−1.32	−1.56	−0.77
Asia	−0.47	−0.49	−0.36	−1.12	−1.17	−0.85
WANA	−0.25	−0.41	−0.66	−0.53	−0.86	−1.39
SSAfrica	−0.40	−0.52	−0.41	−0.84	−1.09	−0.85
Wheat area changes						
LA	0.55	−0.10	−0.12	1.20	−0.20	−0.50
Asia	0.23	0.05	0.01	0.51	0.10	0.02
WANA	0.44	0.28	0.28	0.95	0.61	0.60
SSAfrica	0.24	0.92	1.15	0.52	2.00	2.50
Rice yield changes						
LA	−0.31	−0.52	−0.35	−0.78	−1.31	−0.88
Asia	−0.36	−0.35	−0.27	−0.99	−0.97	−0.71
WANA	−0.30	−0.30	−0.30	−1.20	−1.20	−1.20
SSAfrica	−0.02	−0.16	−0.35	−0.08	−0.57	−1.22
Rice area changes						
LA	0.02	−0.01	−0.01	−0.05	−0.05	−0.05
Asia	0.16	0.03	0.01	0.50	0.10	0.02

Table 3. (Cont'd)

WANA	0.30	0.20	0.20	0.90	0.60	0.60
SSAfrica	0.16	0.65	0.82	0.50	2.00	2.50
Maize yield changes						
LA	−0.14	−0.17	−0.26	−0.47	−0.55	−0.86
Asia	−0.29	−0.40	−0.55	−0.69	−1.02	−1.37
WANA	−0.10	−1.50	−0.20	−0.40	−0.50	−0.80
SSAfrica	−0.07	−0.24	−0.10	−0.13	−0.48	−0.20
Maize area changes						
LA	−0.45	−0.07	−0.18	1.2	−0.20	−0.50
Asia	0.19	0.03	0.01	0.50	0.10	0.02
WANA	0.34	0.22	0.22	0.90	0.60	0.60
SSAfrica	0.19	0.75	0.94	0.50	2.00	2.50
Livestock yield changes						
LA	−0.02	−0.02	−0.02	−0.11	−0.11	−0.11
Asia	−0.02	−0.02	−0.02	−0.11	−0.11	−0.11
WANA	−0.02	−0.02	−0.02	−0.11	−0.11	−0.11
SSAfrica	−0.02	−0.02	−0.02	−0.11	−0.11	−0.11
Livestock herd size changes						
LA	−0.2	−0.2	−0.2	−0.2	−0.2	−0.2
Asia	−0.2	−0.3	−0.3	−0.2	−0.3	−0.3
WANA	−0.2	−0.2	−0.2	−0.2	−0.2	−0.2
SSAfrica	−0.2	−0.2	−0.2	−0.2	−0.2	−0.2

Note: LA – Latin America; WANA – West Asia and North Africa; SSAfrica – Sub-Saharan Africa

For each scenario, these lower yields are inserted into to IMPACT, where they are used to calculate new production levels. The model's supply and demand relationships then determine a new level of prices and consumption, which affect calories consumed per capita, and ultimately human welfare as measured by child mortality.

Results in Table 3 illustrate the yield and area changes under the two scenarios. The simulation results are reported as percentage differences between the base case (i.e., the simulation representing actual changes) and the counterfactual case. Based on the yield contributions described above, yield increases realized under the Green Revolution have been greater than those attributed to the presence of IARCs across the major grain categories. While the IARCs were a major force in the Green Revolution, national agricultural research institutes and other international institutions also made significant contributions. As a reflection of this, the area increases that would happen under lower productivity levels in the counterfactuals (as an alternative way of boosting production) are larger in the no-IARC case than in the case without the Green Revolution. So, we can view the absence of crop technology innovation, in either of the counterfactual cases, as being a missed opportunity for productivity enhancement and savings in cultivated area—with the absence of Green Revolution-induced advances as representing the greater loss of the two.

The design of the counterfactual experiment does not allow for changes in developed countries. Thus, in our simulation experiments, all developed countries realize the actual productivity gains that were observed in this period. The intent of our analysis for developing country regions was to reduce the crop genetic improvement component of crop yields, so as to observe the impacts on overall productivity and crop production resulting from a global equilibrium in all agricultural markets.

The resulting impacts from the changes in crop productivity have significant effects on the global agricultural market equilibrium for the major crops modeled in IMPACT (see Table 4). Reductions in crop production reflect decreases in productivity, and also convey the relative importance of Green Revolution productivity gains relative to the presence of IARCs. The price increases that result from these lower levels of production are also shown, as well as the attendant increases in cropped area and overall trade impacts.

All of these results illustrate that the innovations introduced by CGIs in the 1970s are a key factor that gave rise to the increases in agricultural productivity and production observed during that period. The land that was "saved" by higher crop productivity levels is also reflected here, although other impacts such as the effect on land prices or the substitution for other possible land uses is not shown in our results—as it lies beyond the scope of our modeling framework. But there is no doubt that the labor that would have been locked up in more extensive and less productive agricultural activities would have resulted in decreased earnings from off-farm activities or higher paying non-agricultural sector employment opportunities. This, combined with the higher prices for agricultural produce, would undoubtedly lead to poorer welfare outcomes that would be felt within the wider economy, but which cannot be captured within our partial equilibrium agricultural sector model.

The absence of Green Revolution-generated modern varieties has a much larger effect upon global agricultural markets for grains and livestock, compared to the case in which IARCs are absent (see Table 4). The decrease in global production (and corresponding increase in world mar-

Table 4. Counterfactual-based Effects on Crop Price, Production, Area, and Trade in the Developing World by 2000.

	Wheat	Rice	Maize	Meats	Dairy	All food crops
Global price effects (percent change)						
No Grn Rev	21	47	28	12	11	10
No IARCs	10	17	16	3	2	4
Production effects (percent change)						
No Grn Rev	–15	–10	–28	–8	–10	–10
No IARCs	–7	–4	–14	–2	–1	–4
Area/herd size effects (percent change)						
No Grn Rev	12	12	15	–6	–5	8
No IARCs	5	4	3	–1	–1	3
Net trade effects for the developing world (percent change in imports/exports)						
No Grn Rev	83	27	1,640	–28	–153*	142
Import/Export	*Imports*	*Imports*	*Imports*	*Exports*	*Exports*	*Imports*
No IARCs	34	11	1,143	–3	–15	77
Import/Export	*Imports*	*Imports*	*Imports*	*Exports*	*Exports*	*Imports*

*Change from net exporter to net importer

World Food Policy

Table 5. Impacts on Child Mortality, 1970-2000.

Region	Increase in child deaths ('000 of children)	
	No IARCs	**No Green Revolution**
Latin America	1,540	3,695
Sub-Saharan Africa	1,651	3,703
Middle East-North Africa	333	1,203
South Asia	1,866	6,406
Southeast Asia	3,866	11,592
East Asia	1,390	4,393
All Developing Countries	**10,647**	**30,992**

ket prices) is seen more strongly in the "no Green Revolution" case, and we also see that the increases in cropped area, which is a response to higher prices, are also larger in the case in which Green Revolution productivity improvements are absent. This effect shows a response we would expect when productivity increases are slow or absent, and farmers resort to area extensification in an effort to keep up with growing global demand for food and feed products. Meat and dairy herds and production both decrease in the developing world as production shifts toward the developed world. This leads to a decrease in net exports that originate from these countries. Under the "no Green Revolution" case, we also see that the volume of trade for grains and food crops in general is higher, given that markets try to redistribute food supplies through global trade, so as to supply slower-growing regions with needed food supplies from faster-growing agricultural economies.

While effects on production, prices and other economic variable are both significant as well as interesting to those studying market impacts, the most striking result is the impact on child mortality over time under the alternative scenarios. In the absence of the Green Revolution crop improvements, the number of additional child deaths is estimated at 31 million during the period 1970–2000 (Table 5), or the equivalent of saving 5–10 years of child deaths due to hunger compared to the annual child mortality due to hunger of 3–6 million in 2000, as indicated in the Introduction of this paper. The additional child deaths associated with the no-IARCs case is 11 million. IARCs, or the saving of 2–4 years of child deaths.

The results also show a sizeable effect on child mortality in Southeast Asia, compared to the rest of Asia. While the impact of the no-IARC case had very similar magnitudes for Latin America, Sub-Saharan Africa, and both South and East Asia, the absence of the Green Revolution has a proportionately larger effect in Asia, compared to the other regions. Another counterfactual, which we have not done here, would be to see the impact of a similar green revolution in Sub-Saharan Africa over the same simulation period. No doubt, the impacts of increased agricultural productivity and food availability in Africa would have a similarly striking impact on human well-being measures over the historical period, and could serve to demonstrate how much better off the picture would be, in terms of food security and nutrition, on that continent.

5. Conclusions

The counterfactual analysis that we have shown in this paper demonstrates the importance of the Green Revolution in generating not only sustained improvements in crop productivity growth through the 1970s and 1980s, but also the powerful indirect effects on human welfare as measured by child mortality. The results also confirm the strong supporting role of the IARCs in increasing agricultural productivity and reducing child mortality. The attendant effects on the dynamics of global agricultural markets has also been shown, in terms of production, price, and trade impacts, which are linked to the available calories for consumers and, consequently, to child health, through the feedbacks embodied in the endogenous Dietary Energy Sufficiency relationships.

The regional differentiation of the impacts demonstrated in the counterfactual analyses shown are both reflective of the degree to which crop genetic improvements have actually been embedded in the productivity growth dynamics in those regions, as well as of the nature of the relationships shown by the DES system of growth feedbacks that were estimated across them. Latin America and Africa have less demonstrable effects in terms of productivity growth levels of malnutrition incidence within these counterfactual experiments, which highlights the missed opportunities of the past and underscores the urgency for further embedding the CGIs that were realized through Green Revolution innovations in those regions.

Furthermore, the results of our counterfactual experiments also illustrate the significance of crop improvements attributed to the presence of the IARCs. In fact, the results may underestimate their full impact because the analysis is driven largely by the attribution of productivity gains to either the presence of IARCs or Green Revolution innovation, and do not fully embody the wider benefits that the system of IARCs has brought to agricultural research and innovation systems in the client countries that they have served. It is difficult to capture the strengthening of capacity that has taken place over the years as a result of IARC presence in developing countries, in terms of improvement in research capacity as well as in the efficiency and operation of innovation systems and their integration with national policy and development strategies.

As a concluding thought, it should be noted that both the CGIs realized from Green Revolution-induced technologies and the presence of the IARCs have been key factors in the growth of agriculture in past decades. There is no implied choice of one-over-the-other in the analysis—except to point out that innovations in crop technologies remains the key to sustained productivity growth in those countries most in need of renewal of their food systems. Furthermore, the concurrent improvements in the functioning of crop research and innovation systems can only help this process, but cannot serve as a wholesale substitute to basic crop-level trait advancements.

Our conclusions also address the concerns of some who might argue that the Green Revolution's success in raising basic agricultural productivity levels is offset by environmental impacts of biodiversity losses. From our analysis, there is little doubt that the significant improvements in human well-being that have been realized through the disseminations of improved food crop genetics would be unattainable by other means. The imperative suggested by this research is to further embed these innovations into the agricultural systems of other countries that have yet to fully benefit from the advances observed in South and Southeast Asia. Towards that end, the presence and continued efforts of International Agricultural Research Centers to strengthen capacity and solidify these improvements within national innovation systems will only help and serve as a vehicle for further dissemination and adoption within those regions that are most in need of improvements in agricultural productivity and rural livelihoods.

References

Alston, J.M., C. Chan-Kang, M.C. Marra, P.G. Pardey, and T.J. Wyatt. 2000. "A Meta-Analysis of the Rates of Return to Agricultural R&D: Ex Pede Herculem." IFPRI Research Report No. 113, Washington DC: International Food Policy Research Institute.

Alston, J.M., and P.G. Pardey. 1996. *Making Science Pay: Economics of Agricultural R&D Policy*. Washington DC: American Enterprise Institute for Public Policy.

Avila, A., R. Evenson, S. De Silva, and F. De Almeida. 2003. "Brazil." In *Crop Variety Improvement and Its Effect on Productivity: The Impact of International Agricultural Research*, edited by R. Evenson and D. Gollin. Cambridge, MA, USA: CABI Publishing, 409-25.

Black, R., C. Victora, S. Walker, Z. Bhutta, P. Christian, M. de Onis, M. Ezzati, S. Grantham-McGregor, J. Katz, R. Martorell, and R. Uauy. 2013. "Maternal and Child under Nutrition and Overweight in Low-income and Middle-income countries." *The Lancet* (in press). 382(9890): 427-51. DOI: 10.1016/S0140-6736(13)60937-X).

Brown, L., and H. Kane. 1994. *Full House: Reassessing the Earth's Population Carrying Capacity*. New York: W. W. Norton.

Delgado, C.L., M.W. Rosegrant, H. Steinfeld, S. Ehui, and C. Courbois. 1999. "Livestock to 2020. The Next Food Revolution." 2020 Vision Discussion Paper 28. Washington, DC: International Food Policy Research Institute.

Delgado, C.L., N. Wada, M.W. Rosegrant, S. Meijer, and M. Ahmed. 2003. *Fish to 2020: Supply and Demand in Changing Global Markets*. Washington, DC: International Food Policy Research Institute.

Evenson, R.E. 2003. "Production Impacts of Crop Genetic Improvement." In *Crop Variety Improvement and Its Effect on Productivity: The Impact of International Agricultural Research*, edited by. R.E. Evenson, and D. Gollin, 447-71. Cambridge, MA, USA: CABI Publishing.

Evenson, R.E., and M.W. Rosegrant. 2003. "The Economic Consequences of Crop Genetic Improvement Programmes." In *Crop Variety Improvement and Its Effect on Productivity: the Impact of International Agricultural Research*, edited by R.E. Evenson and D, Gollin, 473-97. Cambridge, MA, USA: CABI Publishing.

FAO (Food and Agriculture Organization of the United Nations). 2002. *The State of Food Insecurity in the World*. Rome: FAO.

Fuglie, K.O., and P. Heisey, September 2007. *Economic Returns to Public Agricultural Research*, Economic Brief Number 10, Washington, DC: USDA Economic Research Service.

Hossain, M., D. Gollin, V. Cabanillay, E. Cabrera, N. Johnson, G. Khush, and G. McLaren. 2003. "International Research and Genetic Improvement in Rice: Evidence from Asia and Latin America." In *Crop Variety Improvement and its Effect on Productivity: The Impact of International Agricultural Research*, edited by R. Evenson, and D. Gollin, 71-108. Cambridge, MA, USA: CABI Publishing.

Huffman, W., and R. Evenson. 2002. "Determinants of State Agricultural Experiment Station Funding Shares." Mimeo.

Huffman, W., and R. Evenson. 2003. "New Econometric Evidence on Agricultural Total Factor Productivity Determinants: Impact of Funding Sources." Mimeo.

Huffman, W., and R. Evenson. 2006. *Science for Agriculture: A Long-Term Perspective*, Second Edition. Ames, IA: Blackwell Publishing.

Hughes, B.B., and E.E. Hillebrand. 2006. *Exploring and Shaping International Futures*. Denver, CO: Paradigm Publishers.

Mitchell, D., and M. Ingco. 1993. *The World Food Outlook.* International Economics Department. Washington, DC: The World Bank.

Pelletier, D., E. Frongillo, D. Schroeder, and J. Habicht. 1995. "The Effects of Malnutrition on Child Mortality in Developing Countries." *Bulletin of the World Health Organization* 73: 443-48. http://www.ncbi.nlm.nih.gov/pubmed/7554015

Rosegrant, M.W., S. Meijer, and S.A. Cline. 2002. *International Model for Policy Analysis of Agricultural Commodities and Trade (IMPACT): Model Description.* Washington, DC: International Food Policy Research Institute. http://www.ifpri.org/themes/impact/impactmodel.pdf.

Rosegrant, M.W., M.S. Paisner, S. Meijer, and J. Witcover. 2001. *Global Food Projections to 2020: Emerging Trends and Alternative Futures.* Washington DC: International Food Policy Research Institute.

Rosegrant, M., and P. Pingali. 1994. "Policy and Technology for Rice Productivity Growth in Asia." *Journal of International Development* 6: 665-88.

Rosegrant, M., and M. Svendsen. 1993. "Asian Food Production in the 1990s: Irrigation Investment and Management Policy." *Food Policy* 18 (2): 13-32.

Scott, G., M.W. Rosegrant, and C. Ringler. 2000. "Roots and Tubers for the 21st Century: Trends, Projections, and Policy Options." 2020 Vision Discussion Paper 31. Washington, DC: International Food Policy Research Institute.

United Nations Children's Fund. 2012. *Levels & Trends in Child Mortality.* New York.

World Education Service Hunger. 2013. *World Hunger and Poverty Facts and Statistics.* Accessed June 29, 2013. http://www.worldhunger.org/articles/Learn/world%20hunger%20facts%202002.htm

A Journal of the Policy Studies Organization
In Collaboration with
The Royal Institute of Thailand

WFP also offers an open, public space with the aim to promote a multi-disciplinary forum for generating conversations on current issues in the food sector around the world. The journal's website (http://www.ipsonet.org/publications/open-access/world-food-policy) is provided for this purpose and the editors warmly invites your contributions, including, commentaries, think pieces, course syllabi, as well as information on food policy-related activities and events. Submissions are welcome at wfpjournal@gmail.com.

WFP
Call for Papers

The editor invites submission of manuscripts contributing to the Journal's Aim and Scope, i.e., to promote a multi-disciplinary forum for generating the analysis and understanding of global trends as well as regional and local forces shaping food and food policies around the world.

Areas of Interest include but are not limited to the following subjects:

- Global or regional trends affecting the production, distribution, and consumption of food
- Policy processes and networks of the national, transnational and global food sector
- Food governance and regulations and effects of these multi-layer institutional mechanisms on food systems
- Political economy of food security and aid
- Food safety, nutrition and health
- Research and development, institutional innovations, and production and consumption alternatives in the food sector
- Rights, accessibility, control and contestations
- Moral and ethical issues in food policy decision and implementation
- Relations and connections between food and other policy issues, such as labor, logistics, energy, environment, and cultural identities

Contributors should consult the author guidelines at http://www.ipsonet.org/images/AuthorGuidelinesWFP.pdf, for manuscript preparation and submission, and http://www.ipsonet.org/publications/open-access/world-food-policy, for more information on the Journal's publication policy.

Submission should be addressed to the editor-in-chief at: WFP.editorial@gmail.com

www.ingramcontent.com/pod-product-compliance
Lightning Source LLC
Chambersburg PA
CBHW081418270326
41931CB00015B/3320
* 9 7 8 1 9 3 5 9 0 7 8 3 1 *